HUMANITY'S
BILL OF RIGHTS

WILLIAM CADWALLADER

ISBN: 1477481567
ISBN 13: 9781477481561
Library of Congress Control Number: 2012909304

CreateSpace, North Charleston, South Carolina

TABLE OF CONTENTS

This book is dedicated to my mom,

the lady who taught me to be the man I am today,

and to my niece and my nephew,

the ones who inspire me to make this world a better place.

PREFACE

Freedom is the right of all sentient beings.

OPTIMUS PRIME

I feel that I have the right to my existence and to be able to make the most out of it. I should not be hindered by the likes of racism, hatred, bigotry, and ignorance. I should not be made to feel less of a person because I do not match someone else's stereotype about my life. My life is my own to lead and the road I take it down is one of my own design. We all have our road that we must follow and it will be different than that of the person next to you or across the world, but just because we all are leading different lives does not mean that we deserve different rights than someone else.

In order to ensure the greatest outcome for every person on this planet, we must all be offered the same rights, privileges, and opportunities. If this is accomplished, we may also find a solution for many of the problems that plague us globally and individually. Only once humanity has put the petty things aside can our time, energy, and resources be used not to destroy those around us but to serve them.

Then let's do it. Plain and simple, let's level the playing field. I have assembled a list of 24 rights, freedoms, and privileges should be made available as a birthright for every member of humanity and the children that spring forth from them - Humanity's Bill of Rights. Every single one of us is entitled to the same rights; regardless of race, gender, sexual orientation, political views, religion, genetics, or any other characteristic humans can think of to discriminate against any sentient being. The freedoms and privileges granted to any one person should be granted to all.

Every day, all across humanity's realm, millions are needlessly deprived of their rights. Many of the problems we face in this world can be traced back to people violating the rights of others. Don't believe me? Sit down one night and watch the news on TV with a copy of Humanity's Bill of Rights in front of you. You will find that most, if not all, of the news stories can be traced back to a violation of one of the listed rights. It is heartbreaking to see how many people run around thinking it is OK to violate the rights of their fellow humans, disrespecting them, violating them, humiliating them, or worse. All the rights listed below are, at least in my eyes, pretty simple and straightforward. Yet it baffles me that some of these rights—rights that I enjoy while living my life—are denied to some.

My own mom taught me a great lesson while growing up: no one is better than anyone else. We are all people, and all people are equal. To me, those are some pretty profound words. She firmly believed that everybody should be allowed to live their own lives and for that I am grateful. Each of us should be allowed to live life the way best suited for him or her and according to his or her own decisions, so long as no harm is done to anyone else. All the people I have ever met have had one thing in common: the will and desire to make their own choices and to not have anyone dictate to them what choices they should make.

We are all children of humanity, all genetic descendants of those who walked this Earth thousands of years ago. Scientists have been able to determine that every person on this planet is descendent of a small band of people that walked the Earth many years ago. Although we are all different—we speak different languages, have different skin tones and different beliefs, and live different lives—we all have the same right to live our lives upon this Earth as we see fit. Some times it can even be mind boggling that physically we are so varied and diverse, but yet we can all trace our genetic roots back in time to the same evolutionary descendents.

I am not going to sit here and talk about how we can all be friends and hold hands and love each other in some utopian love fest, but what I am going to argue for is the simple acceptance that everyone is different from you and yet also the same. If everyone were to treat each other with the same dignity and respect that he or she would also like to be treated with, we could eliminate most of the problems plaguing our planet and our species.

The problems that humanity is facing right now are so vast that they are consuming the lives of millions of people as well as huge amounts of our natural resources. Most of our problems are wars and conflicts that different tribes and groups of humanity are fighting simply because they cannot accept the idea of treating others as they would treat themselves. These are problems based in greed, bigotry, hatred, selfishness, and ignorance.

The consumption of resources by our problems is not only destroying our home here on planet Earth but is also adding to the problems that we humans face. Our environment is nearing total collapse in many areas of our world, many species of planets and animals are either extinct or near extinction, and our population keeps growing while we struggle to find ways to feed it. These are the problems we should be working to solve, not problems based on petty bullshit like whose property line is bigger, who is right, or who has the most oil or on conclusions like "that person thinks differently than I do, so that person must be evil." Many of our avoidable problems arise out of the simple, sad fact that some grown adults don't fully understand they are grown adults and not five-year-old children.

I know many out there are wondering if people of such diversity can live together without war and conflict, if people with such wide-ranging cultures and backgrounds can live together; yet it has already happened and is happening in many places. Let's take Australia as an example—modern-day Australia is a huge melting pot of cultures, with thousands from every corner of the globe immigrating here annually. By many people's thinking, so many different peoples mixing and interacting would mean the country should be one of the most violent places around. This is not the case; most cities in Australia have some of the lowest crime rates around and are annually listed as some of the most livable cities on the planet. I am not saying that Australia is crime-free, but what I am saying is that you can find millions there from every corner of the planet living and interacting, forming communities that are mind-blowingly diverse, and yet most of them can fully accept their neighbors and treat them with the same dignity and respect that they themselves want.

I do believe that if we are to continue to prosper and grow, not only as a species but also as individuals, then we need to seriously rethink a lot of things. We need to grow, get past the petty bullshit we occupy ourselves with, and get on with the important matters at hand. Many of our own people are suffering and being badly mistreated, and our home—our world—is dying a slow and agonizing death because of our own greed and stupidity. Let's take all that we have learned and use that knowledge to better our lives and the world around us. Let's take pride in who we are as a species and work together to build communities and societies that are based upon a solid foundation of respect, freedom, and equality. Fight for what you believe in, but harm none in doing so.

1 - FREEDOM OF SPEECH AND EXPRESSION

all peoples are free to speak openly and honestly through any social medium, including but not limited to written, spoken, and electronically.

If the freedom of speech is taken away then dumb and silent we may be led, like sheep to the slaughter.

GEORGE WASHINGTON

Of all the rights, I will dare to say this is the most important one. Without this right, all the others could not be guaranteed or exist at all. All humans have the need and the right to speak out, say what is on their minds, and be heard. History is full of examples of what great things can happen when people are allowed the freedom to speak and express themselves. Cultures have changed, dictators have fallen, revolutions have been born, leaders of humanity have come about, and so much more, all because of the freedom of speech.

Growing up as a child in the USA, I was taught the Bill of Rights, and one of the rights that stuck out the most to me was the freedom of speech. When it was fully explained to me, I was in awe—there were people out there who actually believed we all should have the right to say what is in our minds and hearts, less we harm none. There were people who believed that we all should be free to write and express ourselves thru whatever medium we choose. That appealed to me so much in fact that it even helped fuel my love for books and writing.

As I grew up and learned more about the world I lived in, it saddened and sickened me to learn that others were dying, losing their lives, and being imprisoned, beaten, and worse for saying what they believed and for pursuing the same right I had been given.

One of the greatest events I have witnessed in my life was the Tiananmen Square protests of 1989. These protests came about because students dared to speak out in a pro-democracy movement in a country ruled by the iron hand of communism, a movement that left hundreds dead or imprisoned. Think about it for a moment—a group of students had such a powerful voice that one of the largest governments in the world feared them and used military force to try to silence them. These students earned the ears of the world.

Most people who know me know that I love to talk. I was given a voice, and I love to use it. I am not always going to be right, but like everybody, I do have a right to be heard and to have my say. I do not believe that I should be silenced by someone else. Furthermore, I believe the same is true for everyone else. I am no better than anyone else on this planet; if I have the right to speak and express myself in my own way, so does everybody else.

Think about this very book—I have devoted many hours to writing it, and I take great pride in it. I want others to read what I have to say and don't want anyone censoring my words or forcing me to write something else because that is what they want me to write. Here is the biggest irony of all of this: I am writing this book while living in a country that does not offer any right to freedom of speech. That isn't even the worst of things, though—as I write this, people elsewhere in the world are being imprisoned and murdered simply for saying what they want or expressing themselves as they choose. "Reporters Without Borders", an international group of journalists and writers, reports that in 2011 sixty-six reporters were killed and another 1066 were arrested for their work.

Giving people the freedom of speech and expression is a means of opening our world up to new sources of knowledge, talent, skill, and innovation. Every work of art ever created, no matter how small, is a clear example of the freedom of speech in action. Go to a bookstore, an art gallery, or a concert, and you are walking into a symphony of voices singing the praises of this freedom. Art and music, just like writing, is an expression what someone else is thinking or feeling and wish to share with the world.

A classic example of this would be the painting titled "Guernica" by the Pablo Picasso in 1937. This massive painting measured over 11 feet in height; with a length spanning over 25 feet. He painted that massive mural after the bombing of the town of Guernica during the Spanish Civil War. Picasso did this to bring the worlds attention to the atrocities that were taking place. It was first unveiled in 1937 at the Paris Worlds Fair and since has become one of his most well-known works.

Another well-known work of free speech would be the song "We are the World". In 1985, a song was created and inspired originally by the famine that took place in Africa during the 1980s that left millions dead. Forty-five of the best known artists, actors, and musicians of the era came together and used their voices to not only speak out about the tragedy, but also to raise money to help those affected and dying from the famine. "We are the World" is one of the best examples of the power that free speech can have and the impact that it can make on the world.

What I want everyone to do is sit back, look a good long look, and think very hard on this. Do you believe the person next to you has a greater right to speak and be heard than you do? Well, speak up now—do you? I certainly don't. We are not always going to agree with what someone else says, but that does not diminish his or her right to speak.

Yes, I know that I maybe opening up a big ol' can of worms. The simple fact of the matter is that not everybody is going to agree with everything that everybody says. Weirdly enough, though, sometimes that just adds to the fun of life. I remember, back in my high school years, I used to have some pretty heated debates with this one guy I went to school with. Some of the debates even happened in the middle of class. But through all of our verbal arguments and debates, we both taught each other the power of freedom of speech. We both had our own opinions, and we were free to express them. Something else we both learned as well as the ability to shut up for five minutes to listen to someone else's point of view.

I could sit here in my chair slamming a drum and hammering on the same topic in twenty zillion different ways, but it all boils down to the same damn thing: we were all blessed with two lips, vocal cords, and awesome minds, all tools that allow us to express ourselves and let the world know who we are and what we think, even if others don't agree. We are all born with the right to speak what we believe, and this is not a right that is to be trampled on by others—we are all members of the same species after all.

2 - FREEDOM OF RELIGION

all peoples are given the freedom to worship as they choose fit so long as it does not interfere with the rights of others. It is also illegal to persecute anyone for his or her chosen beliefs.

It is the position of some theists that their right to freedom OF religion is abridged when they are not allowed to violate the rationalists' right to freedom FROM religion.

JAMES T. GREEN

Well, I am sure that starting this section with that kind of quotation will certainly have a few people running to grab their torches and pitchforks and preparing to hang me from the nearest tree, but wait a second and listen to what I have to say on this. We are all entitled to have our own beliefs and to live our lives as we please. We all at some point look to a higher power, whether it be God, another deity, or enlightenment, and we all need to find the source right for us rather than just be told what is right. We all have to find our own truths in our lives; only we can know what is right for us.

I grew up in a Catholic family, but as I grew up, I found my beliefs differed from those of my family and made my own choices concerning religion. I no longer attend church on Sundays, but I do read the Bible and have learned important lessons from it. I have also studied many other religions and have learned many things from them as well. My mom does not always like my choices, but she respects them because she raised me to do what is right for me. She also believes I am entitled to the freedom to make my own religious choices.

It is that same freedom I am entitled to that I believe all peoples are entitled to. Religion is not a one-size-fits-all solution. Just because something works for you does not mean it is always going to work for me. If it does, fine. But if it doesn't, that is fine, too. It is as simple as that.

It scares me when I watch TV and learn about some countries in the world where religion runs the government and people are forced to live their lives according to a strict religious code because someone in power decided everybody should believe what he believes. I do not think it is a government's place to dictate whom or what people should worship or believe any more than I believe it is a government's job to tell a church how to conduct its business—as long as the church is respecting the Rights of Humanity. I do not believe that it is a government's place to decide for us what to believe or think.

But sadly, there are many on this planet who are so convinced they are right that they feel the need to push their own views on others; to those kinds of people, I say, get over yourselves. No matter what a person says or does, not everyone is going to agree with him or her. To the people who like to hide behind their faiths and use them as a means for denying others their rights, I say, no more. For too long, too many people have hidden behind religion and used it as a battering ram to run over the rights of others. Fair is fair. Like I have said before, all the people on this planet—all the children of humanity—are entitled to all of their rights and not just the ones certain parties think they should have.

Globally there are many countries and regions that have setup theocratic governments based upon religious law. The most famous of these would have to be countries based upon Islamic (Sharia) law. Many of these countries have outlawed other religions, imposed high levels of censorship, strict dress codes, and outlaw most forms of freedom of speech and expression (amongst many other things). I am very thankfully that there are other forms of governments around the world. Most non-theocratic governments do support some level of individual freedoms and do not suppress people and their individuality as much as those based upon some sort of scripture.

We all need to find the path in life that fits us, and that path includes religion. I have a very open-minded view of life, and oftentimes I sit back and watch others go about their lives. It is easy to see how different we all are but also on so many levels the same. We all, at one point or another, ponder our place in the universe and wonder how our own thread of life fits into the fabric of it all. When each of us gets to that point in his or her life, we should all have the right and the freedom to explore that question without fearing persecution, ridicule, humiliation, violence, imprisonment, or worse.

3 - FREEDOM OF EDUCATION AND KNOWLEDGE

all peoples will be allowed to acquire a full education and have equal access to all avenues to education and knowledge. No persons will be penalized for or prohibited from doing so.

The whole purpose of education is to turn mirrors into windows.

SYDNEY J. HARRIS

Due to my family's heavy involvement in the schools as I was growing up, education was seen as something of great importance. I had one uncle who taught for many years, up until his retirement. My mother and her twin sister are both teacher's aides, working with special-needs kids at the local schools. Another aunt also worked as a substitute teacher while also raising four kids of her own. So, needless to say, my family tended not to take things too lightly when it came to the topics of schooling and education.

Because I was surrounded by it so much, I pursued knowledge at every chance and always sought to learn something if I could. I grew up in a small town, and books and knowledge opened doors to new worlds and realms for me. Living in a small town meant very limited avenues to expand my mind and to learn more about the world around me, but my books offered me those opportunities. They took me across the universe, into new frontiers, and even helped me to delve deeper into my own backyard. Books taught me so much. They became my friends in a sense and took me on journeys that allowed me to learn about life, the world, and even about myself. I have always had shelves of books in my home for as long back as I can remember. Books taught me that the impossible is possible. They gave me the knowledge and courage to go out and explore the world and to make the most of it.

It wasn't until later in my life that I learned some people on the planet just don't have the same choices as I do when it comes to knowledge, learning, and education. Some are denied these things because of their social or economic status, gender, or sect or for another of the thousand or so reasons there are. For some, the road to education has a roadblock right in the middle of it. Many of them even use the excuse that it is tradition. Any tradition that forces a person to stay uneducated and not be offered a chance to better themselves is one that needs to change.

Some people really need to wake up and smell the coffee on this topic. The more knowledge and education people have, the better choices they can make for themselves. We never know where the next genius will be found. We do not know what region of the world the next great leader or inventor will be from. Many places have big problems facing them, places like many countries throughout Africa, South America, and the Middle East. There are so many countries throughout these regions and many others with problems ranging from pollution to unemployment, from crime to poverty, from homelessness to injustice. Many of the governments are so self-centered and narrow minded that they fail to see the bigger picture and how empowering their own people could help them tackle and find solutions to their problems by just empowering their people with knowledge.

One of the groups constantly facing a lot of discrimination is females. There are many corners of the globe where females are denied or given severely limited access to education. That just doesn't compute with me. I cannot see any valid reason why this should be the case. When I hear of a group or society denying some of its people an education, I think about how they are just screwing themselves over. The more knowledge people have, the more knowledge that can be put forth to make this world and our cities better places. That person you are denying an education to might just be the very person who can do society the greatest good.

My mom and her family are proof of what educated people, male and female, can accomplish. In fact, their story is nothing special if you really think about it. Stories just like theirs are written every day by families and communities all over the globe, people who have learned the power of knowledge and want to ensure that others have that chance as well. I am talking about people who learn how to take the power of the mind and put it into practice to aid and enhance the world in which they live.

Through the ages, humanity has prized knowledge and even built massive buildings to house its collections of it. The great compendiums of humanity's knowledge are held in the libraries and museums of the world. They range in size from a few small bookcases to mighty complexes that cover many acres. Humans have even been known to leave huge bequests in their wills upon theirs deaths to libraries so others may have the chance to learn and grow. Many public libraries throughout our world and humanity's realm have been funded by simple people who believed in the power of knowledge and education.

Humanity does have some black spots on its soul. There have been times when the storehouses of knowledge were raided and their contents destroyed. In the last one hundred years alone, there have been no less than forty recorded instances of book burnings in addition to countless cases of destructions of schools and institutes of learning. So much of our own history has been lost due to the senseless book burnings. Throughout history humans have gone so far as to destroy entire libraries, many holding irreplaceable works, were destroyed. We can only speculate as to the knowledge they held and how that knowledge could have benefited us all.

I really have to wonder how different life would be in our world if all the books that have been burned and destroyed were still here for us to read and learn from. It was said that the Library of Alexandria in ancient Egypt was one of the most extensive storehouses of knowledge in the world at the time, but sadly, much of that knowledge is now lost to the pages of history. How many books and priceless treasures of humanity's past have been lost to the sands of time. We can only speculate about what we could have learned from them.

Many rulers and regimes have had a big hand in the destruction of knowledge because it suited their own perverted goals. Three names that come to mind are Hitler, Stalin, and the Khmer Rouge. Hitler sought to build up his own perverted ideology by eradicating anyone and anything that did not suit that. Numerous libraries, collections, and treasures were destroyed in very public bonfires. Stalin was well known as a ruthless tyrant who had a direct hand in death of millions and the destruction of any works that were found to be anti-communist. When the Khmer Rouge came to power in the 1970s in Cambodia they wasted no time in changing the entire country into some bizarre Communist society taken back to a primal stage. It is said that over eighty percent of Cambodia's books were destroyed. In addition some of the first people that were targeted for death were doctors, teachers, and highly educated people.

Those are but a few of the many perpetrators of evil out there. Yes I did just say evil because any destruction of knowledge is a crime against all people. Every time we allow books to be burned, schools to be destroyed, and history to be erased, we are further undermining our own people, and by that I mean all people. The knowledge we allow to be destroyed could help to propel us forward. It also could help us learn from the mistakes we have made so we don't make them again. That knowledge could very well be the stuff we need to help solve the problems we face now and in the future.

Instead of fearing knowledge and destroying it, we need to embrace it as something sacred. Knowledge opens doors for us all. It gives us more options and ideas and can help expand the world around us. Instead of limiting knowledge to certain classes and groups, we need to make it available to all peoples, because the person that you ban from learning may just be the person that can solve a great problem.

4 - FREEDOM TO LOVE AND MARRY

a person is allowed to choose his or her own path in matters of love and marriage regardless of any factors, including gender. It is unlawful to force someone to enter into a marriage without his or her openly expressing a desire to do so.

Who, being loved, is poor?

OSCAR WILDE

Growing up in a large family, you learn a lot of things about life, but none is more important than love. I can tell you right away that it takes more than some cosmic strings of the universe to bond so many people together. It is only natural that when you do know love you want to enjoy more of it and if you are really lucky, find someone special to share it with. To know what it is to love and be loved is one of the greatest things ever. No more can we control the bonds that create love than we can control whom the person we love or are loved by is.

That person may be from another town, another village, another country, another social class, another religion, or another culture—so what? None of that means anything when it comes to matters of the heart. I do believe that any time two willing people come together in the act of love, it is a good thing, regardless of all other factors.

We have songs sung about it, movies made about it, and books written about it. One of the most famous texts about love is *Romeo and Juliet*, written by the immortal William Shakespeare. This timeless tale tells us about two lovers who are so determined to be together that they end up joining each other in death. This story is a bit over-the-top and morbid, but it also shows us what lengths people will go to in the name of love.

According to some ancient legends and myths, even wars have been fought over love. One of the most powerful legends revolving around love is that of the "Sacred Band of Thebes," a military group from the fourth century BC that consisted of 150 male couples. The reasoning behind the makeup of this special unit was that no man would disgrace himself in front of his beloved. The sacred band last for forty years before it was defeated, but no one ever surrendered, each instead falling beside his love.

Love can be pretty powerful stuff. Yet for all the good it does our world, there are many who even today deny others the right to love whom they wish. In some parts of the world, you are not allowed to love or marry someone outside of your own social class (that's a pretty popular one). In many parts of the world, especially in many areas of the United States, it is a taboo to marry someone who isn't the same skin color as you. Another one that is pretty common is a taboo in many religious circles where it is unacceptable to love someone outside of your own religion. There are even recording showing where it was unacceptable in many royal families to marry someone that was not noble born.

Those who deny others the right to love and marry usually use many tools in their arsenal of evil to back their arguments, the most common one being the Bible. Oftentimes they take one sentence from that book that best backs their argument, even if there are twenty others that contradict it. What is the point of all of this? Why fight something so wonderful as love? Why make laws and false arguments to fight something that does a lot of good for the world and the people involved?

My marriage is one such relationship. My husband and I have been together for years, but in order to get to where we are now, we had to move to another country—my own would not recognize our relationship in any way, shape, or form. Even then it wasn't a walk in the park: we fought hard against a bureaucracy that had it in its mind that our relationship wasn't real and that did everything it could to find flaws, even forcing me to return back to my own country to continue the fight. In the end we won our battles and have been together through thick and thin for over eight years now. It has not all been easy—in fact, there have been times when it has been tiring—but I do feel I am a better person for being in love with and being loved by my husband. Being loved by him makes me want to be a better person and to do what I can to see him smile at the end of the day, and it makes the world a better place.

One problem we face as a couple is that our government does not officially recognize our relationship for what it is—a loving marriage. They instead call it a partnership, and if one of us dies, the other of us must face amazing odds that most other widows and widowers would never have to face. That is just plain wrong. I do believe that what laws protect one couple should apply to all loving couples, regardless of any other factors. Who are we as mere humans to dictate to each other what type of relationships are right or wrong? My relationship is perfect for me, but that does not mean it should be for all. All people need to be allowed the freedom to make their own choices regarding their relationships.

If humanity is to survive, one thing we need to do is widen our viewpoints on the world, including about relationships. We need to look beyond our own backyard and look at the diversity that human relationships come in. In some parts of the world, it is culturally acceptable for a man to have more than one wife, yet in many Western countries it is against the law. That type of relationship is not my thing, but if it is right for others, who am I to judge? Relationships are like flavors of ice cream: one flavor is right for some but may not be right for others.

We must keep in mind, though, that with the freedom to love and marry must come the freedom to choose the terms of one's relationships, and that includes being able to choose to leave a relationship. Relationships, like people, change over time; some would even say that they evolve. Sometimes the changes are for the better, but sometimes they aren't. It has been said that people fall into as well as out of love. I have been in many relationships over the years, and for one reason or another most have ended. In fact, I do not know what the future holds for the one I am in now, but as long as the love is there, I am going to enjoy it. If the day does come when the relationship ends, I will enjoy the freedom to move on, just as I enjoy the freedom to love whomever I choose. These are the same freedoms I strongly believe all people are fully entitled to.

Marriage is one of the most widely debated topics around, and why exactly it is beats the hell out of me. What marriage boils down to is the ultimate bonding between two people (in some cases more). Many hold on to the old and outdated belief that marriage is strictly between a man and a woman. I do not believe this is relevant anymore. Marriage, like relationships and life itself, needs to change and evolve to meet the needs of the times, not of ages long ago. What really matters is not the who of a relationship but the love that brought the people together. It is that love and the freedom of people to love whomever they wish that needs to be protected. Love is one of the most powerful forces on this planet and every person deserves to love and be loved.

5 - FREEDOM TO BE

each person is allowed to be the person of his or her own choosing. All people are allowed to make the decisions concerning their own lives and bodies. No one shall ever be persecuted for being the person of his or her own choosing as long as doing so does not interfere with the rights of others.

He who trims himself to suit everyone will soon whittle himself away.

RAYMOND HULL

"Just be yourself," Mom always said—easier said than done. It seems like every time we turn around we are faced with others wanting us to fit their molds and ideals. No biggie—this is in itself a part of being a human—but so is the freedom of being able to explore and be the person you want to be, not the person someone else thinks you should be. OK, I admit that the "freedom to be" is one of the vaguest on the list, but still, it is in my opinion one of the most precious rights. Instead of being forced to fit someone else's idea of what we should be or become, we all need the freedom to choose and decide for ourselves who we are.

When I was seventeen, I was living in a small town in Louisiana and just beginning to discover who I was. At the same time, I was also discovering that the town I was living in was not all that friendly toward people like me. After much soul-searching, I figured out that in order to be me, I had to leave that town, and so I did. I followed my dreams and moved to the West Coast to live with my dad. For me, that was the best move of my life because it allowed me to explore who I was and who I would decide to become. That journey opened my eyes to world beyond my wildest imagination. To this day I even refer to it as the journey that started it all.

By making that change—by choosing to be the person I wanted be and knew I could be—I set upon my own road and made my own choices about my life and how I was going to live it. What enabled me to do this the most was the promise that I would have the chance and the freedom to discover who that crazy guy running around inside of me was. I must say that it was a fun journey. It was not an easy journey, but it was mine and one that I would never trade for anything. It was a journey that took me from the Deep South of Louisiana to the great Pacific Northwest and then on to the beautiful, sun-drenched land of Melbourne, Australia. Without being able to enjoy the freedom to be, I would neither have learned so much about myself nor been able to meet so many people and have so many great experiences.

I do believe I was one of the lucky ones. There are many people around the world who are forced to fit exactly into the pegs etched out for them by their families or cultures, without ever being able to truly explore being the people they desire to be and were meant to be. This approach to life is not healthy, and it does not do anyone any real good. When a person is forced to walk a path in life that someone has set out for them and that they do not wish to travel, they are really suppressing themselves and denying the world what could be a gem instead of a run-of-the-mill lump of coal.

I am not going to limit this discussion to one about life's goals and careers, but I will narrow it down to being human. I have faced many critics who have claimed being gay was a choice, like one were picking out a breakfast cereal, but that is far from the truth. It is a part of who I am and also why I had to make some choices in my life, but it was not a choice in itself. The only choice I had was whether or not I was going to accept who I was and embrace me or hide it and live a life of denial and regrets. Ask anyone who truly knows me, and he or she could tell you that I march to the beat of my own drum in life.

I live my life to make me happy and to fulfill myself. I know, that makes me sound like a selfish asshole, but we do need to put ourselves first in many ways because no one else will. Sure, life has been trying at times, but I was always proud of the fact that I was living my life and living with the choices I made. I will admit that some of my choices were less than stellar, but they were mine and I made them. I did not let someone else decide for me what I was going to be or how my life will be lived - that is my choice and my right.

One incident that sticks out in my mind on this topic is from a recent episode from the TV show *Glee*, in which the character Mike deals with the very struggle to have the freedom to be. His father had decided for him that he was going to make straight As and attend Harvard, when that was not what he wanted for himself. He wanted to be a dancer and strived to be the best dancer he could. It finally came to a head when his mother confronted him and he told her the truth. She supported his choice to be a dancer because she herself had made her decisions on whom she wanted to be on the basis of pleasing others, and she lived with the regrets from that.

Another recent incident in which someone's freedom to be was clearly violated has to do with the actress Marzieh Vafamehr, star of the film *My Tehran for Sale*. She was recently sent to jail for one year and also sentenced to ninety lashes for appearing on camera without her government-required religious headgear. She is one of the lucky ones, however, as her country folded to international pressure and released her after only ninety days. She has to practice her acting craft underground, but she isn't alone. She is like many others in her home country of Iran and elsewhere. Dancers, artists, actors, writers, and more have to hide who they really are because they are banned from their craft, their art. It is sad that such talented people, who can bring so much joy and fun to life, cannot be themselves.

Prisons around the world are filled with people whose only crime was trying to express their freedom to be. All they wanted was to be the people they saw inside themselves. For many of us, the idea of being imprisoned for this is unfathomable, but it is happening. People have been imprisoned for loving someone, for thinking for themselves, for expressing their creativity, for speaking their minds, or for any number of other reasons that the over-controlling, heartless dictatorships and military governments of the world might feel threatened by them.

I cannot imagine a world without dance, music, art, and movies. It may be a slightly selfish point of view to some, but I enjoy the results of great people expressing their freedom to be, their freedom to express themselves in the forms of their choosing. That also results in my being able to enjoy more of my freedom to be—to be entertained, informed, pushed mentally, and able to look at my world through a new viewpoint.

If a person's journey through life to be leads them to be a dancer, artist, writer, doctor, teacher, or even traveler to another land; whatever it maybe then we must be allowed to take those roads that best suit us and our life, less we harm none. Most of the great discoveries that have shaped humanity throughout history have come about because people took control of their own lives and made their own choices, not because they allowed someone to make their choices for them. If people had not taken advantage of their freedom to be and forged their own paths, we would not have had explorers like Magellan and Columbus; visionaries like Bill Gates and Steve Jobs, who have changed the way we communicate and interact with the world around us; or such amazing filmmakers as George Lucas and Steven Spielberg. And I would not be the person I love to see looking back at me when I look in the mirror.

In researching for this book, I stumbled upon many cases of governments violating people's freedom to be. One that stuck out to me was the case of Banda Aceh. A group of youths there who choose to follow the punk subculture routinely have their rights violated because of some Bible-thumpers in the government who believe everybody should follow Sharia law, even if that means denying him or her the chance to learn, speak freely, and be the person of his or her own choosing. Many of these youths are forcibly reeducated against their own wishes. Make no mistake: I am not talking about an isolated case, but rather situations like this are common all over the world. I have even seen stuff like this happen in the United States. Why don't you report on that sometime, CNN?

Learning and discovering what life is about is never an easy task. We all face our own trials and tribulations. Along the ways we do have many wonderful and exciting things embark special memories and feelings upon us. We socialize, make friends, have lovers, and loved ones. Every life lived throughout history and in the days yet to be is a unique individual who will lead a life different then that of any other person. By having the Freedom to be, we are giving people the freedom to be the best person they can, less we harm none.

6 - FREEDOM TO ELECT
GOVERNING BODIES

all people over the age of eighteen are allowed to cast votes for the elections of their lawmakers and governing officials. This also gives all people the right to run for election without unfair costs, penalties, or persecution.

I am neither bitter nor cynical but I do wish there was less immaturity in political thinking.

FRANKLIN D. ROOSEVELT

If history has taught us anything, it is that more often than not, rulers who are not kept in check can end up being a bad thing, not only for the people they rule but also for many others on this planet. Growing up, I learned that the purpose of a government was to run a country, to protect it and its people, and to make laws to help people go about living their lives. It was only later that I learned how things can go badly.

One of the most infamous governments was that of Hitler, a man who started out as an elected official but decided he was above being elected and became a dictator. He then went on a megalomaniac streak and took over many other countries over the course of his reign. We all know what happened after that—World War II, millions dead, and cities and lives left in ruin. He played the role of a showman and he did it well. So well in fact that he was able to convince his followers that murdering Jews, gypsies, homosexuals, and anyone they saw as a scapegoat or a threat to their power.

Hitler is one example of how things can go badly when a man goes from being an elected official to a power-hungry dictator. We have many examples in our own times of such men—Gaddafi (Libya), Mobutu (Zaire), Kim Jong-il (North Korea), and Castro (Cuba). There are many countries in the world where dictatorships still reign and rulers still rule with an iron fist, such as Burma, Equatorial Guinea, Somalia, Sudan, Tibet, Turkmenistan, Uzbekistan, and Zimbabwe. That list is by no means comprehensive. There are also many peoples who are only as free as the leash their rulers keep them on allows. Many Arab countries fit such a bill. According to Wikipedia, almost two billion people live under dictatorships or non-democratic governments.

Well, in my book that is two billion too many, two billion who don't have the opportunity to give their voices to discussions of how their country should be run and what laws should govern them. People should be free to choose their government officials. People should also be free to remove these officials from office if they don't fulfill their duties or meet the needs of the people they were elected to serve. Laws that are fair and just and allow people to live their lives to the fullest without others dictating to them, telling them what they must do, how to act, and what to believe.

In many countries, it is a small group of people with its own agenda and narrow-minded ideas that runs the show and calls the shots. These are the same people who also use every trick in the book and commit many unthinkable acts to stay in power, the same people who put their own needs, wants, and desires ahead of those they rule. The end results of such governments' rule litters our world's history books as well as our modern newspapers. Many of these places also end up covered in the bodies of the dead, which include the innocent, the literate, the opposition, protesters, and some who just wanted to help others.

I firmly believe that if humanity is to survive, it is very important for the governments of all nations to assure and look after humanity's rights. All nations must be allowed to hold free elections, and all people must be allowed to choose the bodies that govern them. Those bodies must be fair and equal, not partial to any one group.

Growing up, my mom always said, "What you do for one, you do for all." Simply put, if you show favoritism, you are sowing the seeds of descent and growing a garden of problems. That right there is the fatal flaw of many so-called governments around the world. They favor special interest groups or certain groups of people, leaving many others out in the cold without voices of their own. Those without a voice in how their governments and their lives are run become disgruntled, angry, bitter, and resentful.

Many, many times over, those same people without a voice in their governments take matters into their own hands. We all have seen this happen, especially in recent times. Two modern examples of this are Libya and Egypt. In both cases, people had had enough and forced the downfalls of the governments in power, but not without bloodshed. This was bloodshed that would not have needed to happen had all the people been given a voice in their governments and the ability to elect officials rather than be forced to put up with tyrants who felt they were above being elected.

Now, I know some are going to start asking about the kings and queens of the world, those famous and infamous families we all know about and read about in the papers and tabloids. Well, let us set the record straight— there are very few monarchs left in the world, and most of them are only figureheads or the heads of constitutional monarchies where most of the true running of the country is done by parliaments and other elected officials. Denmark and England are two of the most well-known examples of constitutional monarchies.

A true government is one that is elected by its people to tend to affairs of state and civil matters. A government should not be putting its nose into the personal lives and freedoms of its people. It is not a government's job to tell its people what to believe and who they should be. A true government serves the people; the people do not serve the government like slaves. A true government does what is in the best interests of all the people, not what is in the best interests of themselves or their financial backers. It is not a government's job to bleed the people dry like they are walking and talking cash machines, and the people are also not to be cannon fodder for the government's petty wars.

7 - RIGHT TO EQUAL ACCESS OF
MEDICINE

all people have the right to seek medical treatment. All people have equal access to all forms of medical treatment, including Western, preventative, alternative, herbal, nature-based, and any other form of treatment that is part of a person's culture.

No man is a good doctor who has never been sick himself.

CHINESE PROVERB

We all get sick at one time or another in our lives. Whether our egos will let us admit it or not, every person at some point needs medical help. In this modern world, the avenues for medicine are as wide and diverse as the types of trees in our forests. Many of us only think about Western medicine, the land of pills and potions, doctors and nurses, surgeries and trauma, but there are many different types of treatments and therapies out there.

Some of the many treatments available include aromatherapy, acupuncture, aquatic therapy, acupressure, herb remedies, chiropractic, crystal therapy, cupping, massage therapy, yoga, body wraps, iridology, shiatsu, light therapy, meditation, reflexology, ozone therapy, Pilates, and Reiki. Keep in mind that these are just a few of the "alternative" treatments and therapies in the world today. Many of them show better results for certain things than Western medicine does.

One of the more well-known of these would be chiropractic. Many people with back issues can attest to its effectiveness. Simple yet calculated manipulations of certain vertebrae can alleviate and even cure many aliments of the skeletal system without the use of surgery or pills. After a back problem in 2001, I was left in serious pain and also had movement issues. I sought the help of a chiropractor for some relief. After only two treatments, I was left feeling on top of the world and as if nothing had ever happened to me.

Another one that many people are aware of is yoga, made more famous by its swarms of celebrity practitioners. The form of yoga best known to the Western world is actually called hatha yoga. Some of its more famous practitioners include Madonna, Ricky Martin, and Jennifer Aniston. It has been proven to offer real benefits to people's health and overall well-being. The sad thing is that in many Muslim sects, yoga is banned due to the belief that it has Hindu origins and that it is therefore blasphemy and will erode the faith. This deprives many people of a beneficial treatment that could offer them real health benefits. Not to be outdone, the Vatican has also officially taken a disapproving stance toward yoga and meditation, but unlike Islamic countries, it has not made a ban the law of the land. I know many people of different faiths who practice yoga, and they do not see it as something that will destroy their faith but rather as something that will make them healthier and stronger.

One form of medical research that has been widely debated in recent times is stem cell research, which could revolutionize medical treatments around the world for cancer, muscular damage, Parkinson's disease, spinal cord injuries, multiple sclerosis, and more. The treatments arising from stem cell research are still in their infancy compared with many other forms of treatment, but they have the potential to open up new doors. Many countries have banned stem cell research on the grounds of falsehoods. Many believe that stem cells can only come from human embryos, but that is not that case. Scientists have a variety of ways now that they can extract stem cells without causing any damage to human (or potential human) life. I do believe this is an area we need to proceed into with caution, but I do not believe our caution should stop us from developing treatments that could greatly enhance the lives of millions around the world. Scientists all over are hard at work studying and finding new ways to use stem cells for treatments.

Stem cells have already been used successfully in bone marrow transplantation, and that is only the beginning. A recent report out of England stated that Professor Marc Turner from Edinburgh University is working to create artificial human blood from stem cells. Professor Turner's research could end blood shortages worldwide and resultantly solve many problems for many nations, because even many of the most advanced countries routinely face shortages of blood supplies. In many third world countries, safe and healthy blood supplies are not possible to maintain or do not exist, leading many people to die needlessly.

One of my favorite therapies is a good ol' massage. Nothing else compares with having your muscles fully worked over, eliminating built-up stress and getting your juices flowing. I know firsthand the benefits of massage therapy. Growing up, I was always a hyper, high-strung kid and could drive people crazy. Many nights, in order to calm me down, my mom would just start rubbing my back, and in a short amount of time I could go from high-strung to mellow. My mom certainly was no fool. She had found a simple and effect method to calm a child with mild ADHD: not pills but just a massage. In today's world, humans are faced with more stress than ever, and a massage is a simple and holistic method for dealing with stress issues and also improving people's health and mental well-being.

In researching for this chapter, I contacted several dear friends of mine who are involved with holistic therapies and alternative treatments. The first one I contacted was Dr. Craig Ledwell, a respected acupuncturist in Louisiana. He was trained in China and learned the classical Chinese methods of acupuncture. Since he first started his practice, he has gone beyond his original training and has even learned a little-known form of acupuncture called Microsystems. Dr. Ledwell spent quite a bit of time over the years I have known him talking and educating me on many areas of acupuncture and herbal medicine.

Another form of treatment that Dr. Ledwell has been working with is actually one that little has been published about, but it is very revolutionary. It is called Colorpuncture, and it was developed by Peter Mandell over the course of twenty-five years. This treatment revolves around the use of color and light to treat aliments in a similar fashion to acupuncture. Both of them revolve around the use of meridians, or energy pathways, in the human body. Colorpuncture accomplished this without any needles or invasive treatment. It is more complex than that, but that is the basis of it. During my talks with Dr. Ledwell, he told me that everyday he meets someone who has been let down by traditional medicine, someone who has grown disillusioned with the "here's a pill" mentality that now runs rampant like a deadly disease through many doctors' offices and hospitals globally.

Even I have been treated by Dr. Ledwell using his color punch therapy. Several years ago I was in a car accident that left me with emotional trauma. For a few months, I battled the aftereffects of the car wreck. My emotions were totally out of balance and even had severe trouble interacting with people. It wasn't until I went home for a Christmas holiday that I visited Dr. Ledwell. When I told him about the problems I was having, he offered me a treatment. I figured it was worth a shot even if it could be a crock of bullshit. The treatment lasted thirty minutes, and afterward I truly felt like my old self again. I went into the treatment a skeptic with nothing to lose, but I left the room felling like a new man.

Someone else who I contacted in the course of the research for this book is another longtime friend of mine who was Edgar Louviere, a nurse at a doctor's office. I spoke with him openly and honestly about the doctor he works with and the current state of Western medicine as he sees it on a daily basis. Mr. Louviere and the doctor he works for, Dr. Roland Degeyter, are two men of a dying breed in traditional medicine in the United States. They truly believe in working to treat the ailments and problems of the patients. They have managed to avoid the halfhearted pill-popping approach to medicine that many so-called doctors now take. Instead of treating patients and trying to get to the source of the problems, many doctors apart from these two would rather crank you up on pills until something happens to work.

Mr. Louviere takes a very unusual approach to his work in medicine because he is a strong advocate for alternative and nontraditional medicine. Mr. Louviere is the person who first introduced me to Dr. Ledwell. At the time, he was working part-time with Dr. Ledwell to develop a range of herbal remedies based on traditional Chinese herbal formulas. The formulas they worked with had a long history behind them, and they were even adamantly against the use of animal products in the herbal remedies they were marketing at the time.

In the past few decades, herbal remedies and treatments have become very popular and some might even say trendy. I was first introduced to all of this back in 1993 by Barbara Teufert, the mother of a good friend of mine. This amazing lady had been working with herbs and holistic remedies for many years before I even met her. In recent years she has even turned me toward peoplespharmacy.com, a website she visits often. Her work and success rate with natural remedies is so good that it is very rare for her to take any member of her family to a doctor. She even has many friends who consult her for advice. She is looking forward to publishing a book based on her work, remedies, and treatments sometime in the near future.

One form of herbal remedy that has been in the news frequently in recent years has been marijuana. Marijuana has a long and badly tainted history, thanks in part to poor information. If people get past the stigma and the views they learn from pop culture, they could actually see what it can do to help people. A few places around the world have woken up to this fact and have accepted that marijuana can be an aid to some people as an alternative to the standard pill-popping and chemical ingestion of typical Western medicine. I personally know of many people who choose marijuana to help them with medical issues. These issues range from cancer to insomnia to arthritis and beyond. I am not talking about people who sit around and spend their days getting shit-faced but rather people who have families and jobs and choose a natural herbal remedy as a form of treatment.

These are only a few different therapies and treatments in our world. There are so many in existence now and more yet to come that we have not even thought of. People should be allowed free access to the medical treatment that best suits them, even if we may not always agree with some of the choices people make. In my own life, I have been faced with medical issues just like everyone else, but I am grateful I was allowed to decide for myself what roads I would take. There were times when traditional medicine fit the bill, but there were other times when I turned to nontraditional treatments.

The ultimate decision on a person's health lies with each of us and not with the government. We all have the right to decide what works for us, and we do not need the government passing laws that hinder this right. We are talking about our bodies, which we inhabit during all of our time on Earth. We are allowed to choose how our bodies should be nourished, so why should it be any different when it comes to our health and medical care?

For all the treatments out there, many are denied access to medicine and treatment for illnesses and ailments. Globally, there are millions who are denied access to treatments for one reason or another. Some are denied them because of their gender, race, social class, ethnic background, or sexual orientation or for another of a number of screwball reasons people come up with. In many countries of the world, women are still treated like second-class citizens in every aspect of their lives, from education to health. In other countries, certain sectors of society are denied many of the basics of life because they do not belong to the right political or ethnic group.

As many instances in human history have shown us, if we do not take care of ourselves and those around us, including when it comes to health, things can become unstable; but if people are healthy and happy, prosperity follows. Health care should not be preserved for the privileged few, because this only leads to resentment. The people who are denied treatment may just end up being the same people you need the most, but by denying them access to medicine, you lose out. Medicine is not a one-size-fits-all sort of thing but needs to be used and thought of on a more human basis.

8 - RIGHT TO PRIVACY

all people are entitled to privacy. This includes in their homes and while using their personal electronic devices.

> *If the right to privacy means anything, it is the right of the individual, married or single, to be free from unwarranted governmental intrusion.*
>
> WILLIAM J. BRENNAN

We share many parts of our lives with others, but there are also parts we wish to keep to ourselves. There is not one person on this planet who does not have something about themselves that they want to keep to themselves. That, my friends, is a part of nature. Love it or loathe it, we all have our secrets and we don't have the right to strip others of theirs. If someone wishes to hold a secret that harms none, I do believe it is his or her choice and no one else's to do so.

In today's age of technology, the Internet, and computers, it is hard to forget that such a thing as privacy exists because it is so easy to report on the activities of others. It is for that very reason, though, that it is more important than ever for us to respect privacy and be reminded that it is a freedom all people deserve. Cameras are so readily available to us thanks to our wonderful techno toys, and if what you shoot is good enough or invasive enough, there is always someone willing to pay you money to see it. Read any magazine these days and you'll see that it looks like a giant game of "who can get the bigger secret." Some even go so far as to make up the secrets if they cannot get any real ones.

Just because we can do something does not always mean we should. The very people we are aiming our cameras at are also our neighbors and our families, and by doing so, we are also giving them every right to point their cameras back.

No person enjoys having his or her life under a microscope. By giving people the freedom of privacy, you are also giving people the freedom to think, create, and build without harm or intrusion. I know many creative-minded people who work best when they are left alone in their privacy to create without any outside influence. I have also experienced this firsthand while writing this book. While writing, I actually did not tell many people about the book or my ideas, and those that I did tell kept my secrets for me. I think that my work as a writer is better for being allowed the privacy I needed to think and create. When I am writing, I will sometimes go so far as to lock myself in my home office for hours on end and speak to no one. It is my choice to do this because it is my creation—my work—and I have the right to do with it what I will.

Quite often the reasons we desire privacy is because of our families. For most people on this planet, their family is the group with which they will share the strongest and most important bond they ever will have, and that bond includes its fair share of secrets. Those secrets could be about many things, from personal struggles to private shames. I have seen family secrets go so far to be concealed that only a select few know of them and do not tell anyone else out of a concern for protection and safety. I personally partici-pated in sharing a secret like this several years ago, when a deep secret came to light in my husband's family. It came out that one of my husband's aunts had given a daughter up for adoption many decades ago. This had been kept a secret because of social circumstances at the time it happened. Due to social stigma, she was forced to hide her pregnancy and gave her daugh-ter up for adoption. This ladies right to privacy allowed her the freedom to handle a tough situation on her own terms. Sometimes in life we are dealt horrors, trials, tribulations, or any number of other things that we must face and deal with, but privacy allows us to come to terms with them. Who better is there to help than those close to us?

Governments are the masters of hypocrisy when it comes to privacy. With regard to their own events and affairs, they demand a high level of secrecy and privacy, but with regard to the lives of those they govern, it is a different story. Most governments are so paranoid about staying in power that they do not have any problem finding ways to invade the privacy of others. The US government is a classic example of this with its Department of Homeland Security, a government office that makes it its mission to invade privacy under the cover of protecting the people. It is not the only one. I have no doubt in my mind that every government on this planet is guilty of this.

Recently in the media, electronics have come under fire because many governments all over the world feel that people's right to privacy does not extend to their stuff, including their phones and electronic gizmos. I do not believe that this is the case. We all need to have safe places where we can keep our secrets safe, whether it be a diary or an iPhone. I remember as a kid my mom gave me a journal and encouraged me to write in it. She told me it was a man's version of having a diary. Under most countries laws that journal was protected under law. Now that journal can be found in my electronic toys and aids. This can be saide ofr most people in our modern times. This wonderful technological wonders have allowed us to take our journals

Currently there are at least 8 recorded cases in the USA for 2012 that has an iPhone listed in a search warrant, nicknamed "iWarrants". In the time since late 2007, more then 50 cases have been found where an iPhone is named in a search warrant. These statistics and more information was recently brought to light in a tech article written by John Jeff Roberts, published in May of 2012. In 2011 California governor Jerry Brown vetoed Senate Bill 914; which would have made it illegal for cops to search an iPhone without a warrant.

Privacy and the secrets it allows to be kept are the key to many innovations and discoveries. Many writers, artists, scientists, and creators use
privacy to make their visions fully come to life. It doesn't matter if you are
ordinary or extraordinary, we are all entitled to privacy. By doing so we are
also allowing ourselves to safeguard that part of our world that could help
define us. I don't believe privacy is a bad thing, it really boils down to what
we make from our privacy that matters the most.

9 - RIGHT TO TRIAL BY JURY

all persons accused of a crime are entitled to a speedy trial by a jury of their peers.

Hunger makes a thief of any man.

PEARL S. BUCK,

You Said a Mouthful

S hit happens, plain and simple. Sometimes one moment in our lives can drastically change things for us. It can be by our own design or because of someone else. Many of us, at some point in our lives, will find ourselves in a courtroom. When this does happen, we want to be assured we will be treated with decency and fairness. One of the best ways to do this is to ensure people can get a fair trial by a jury of their peers.

When trouble does find us, there are certain things we all want—good legal advice, honesty, justice, and a fair go. One of the best ways these can be attained is through a working legal system where trials by juries are used to safeguard the rights and liberties of the people. Many times a jury can even save good people from unjust laws or laws that are turned around and used unfairly.

All of the juries I have ever seen are made up of ordinary people, not lawyers or legal specialists. A member of a jury could be someone's mom, dad, brother, sister, or neighbor; when it comes to a jury, you just never know who will be on it, and that is the way it should be. The jury should consist of open-minded individuals who aren't prejudiced but have brains and consciences. In a courtroom, everyone has his or her own biases and prejudices, but a good jury is willing to ignore each side's biases and even the judge's and make a solid decision based upon the facts and its conscience.

When a person faces legal troubles, he or she hopes for several things: due process, decency, to be a treated as a person and not a sideshow, not to be humiliated, access to sound legal advice, and fairness. What is so hard about guaranteeing someone all these things? To me they sound like the simplest things anyone could ask for. Level out the playing field—bring back fairness and equality. Legal processes should neither be a source of entertainment nor fuel for political goals for those in power.

In the world we live in now, millions do not have any access to either a proper legal system or the tools to defend themselves in it, not even in the United States. All too often, people get trampled on and destroyed even by a legal system that was meant to protect them. Oh, hell, let's be honest, in prisons worldwide there are people doing time simply on an accusation without any due process or legal avenues available to them. One of the greatest examples of this is Guantanamo Bay, a prison being used to house people accused of terrorist acts. Sadly, most of the imprisoned here have never seen the inside of a courtroom or even faced any formal changes beyond having a finger pointed at them. If they are guilty of committing crimes, let them be formally charged and then deal with the punishments they are entitled to, but if they are not, get them out of their cages and let them go about their lives.

Others groups that have notorious histories of violating people's rights are the communist regimes of the former Soviet Union and China. One of the many examples that the former Soviet Union has to offer in the realm of violating people's rights is a jury trial that took place during the Stalin government. It was a time in history when millions were sentenced to harsh imprisonments and even death with no trial and for no reason. The government fed off of the fear of its people and turned neighbors and even families against each other. Many turned in others on false charges, but that made no difference to the authorities. All someone had to do was just say something and the person or persons they accused would be put to death or put on a one-way train to Siberia. Many people sent to Siberia never made it there, dying horrific deaths along the way. Those who did make the dangerous journey were still forced to endure unbelievable hardships and tortures.

The record of modern-day China is just as stained as that of the former Soviet Union. Most times, people accused of violating the law there never see the inside of a courtroom before they are dragged off to one of the state-run prisons. These prisons have a well-documented history of being nothing more than slave labor camps where these people produce cheap goods and are tortured and made to deal with inhuman conditions until they drop dead. Very few people make it out of these prisons alive. Even though China has some good spin doctors and can weave some good tales to cover its tracks, the facts remain—its prisons and work camps are filled with prisoners serving severe sentences who have never been on trial for a crime.

During my research for this book, I stumbled on a report that states that in Beijing the government is cracking down on security companies that run illegal "black jails." Many of these companies imprison people who come to Beijing to put a petition to the government. These security companies make a big business out of these illegal jails and prison facilities. Many believe closing these illegal prisons is only a small step, but it still important for people. Many people go to Beijing every year to petition for various things and improve their lives, and it is sad when such people only end up facing illegal detention at the hands of money-hungry sadists.

If history has shown us anything in this area, it is that justice is something that must be fought for, held on to tightly, and never taken for granted. Justice must be fair, compassionate, and just. There are always people out there who would pervert it or use it to hide their own evils. If we as a people are to build a foundation of rights for all to live and be equal, we must also have a system of justice that is fair and unbiased for all people and not just those who have enough money or influence to buy their way around it. Fair is fair. No more lying, no more cheating, fair is fair.

10 - PROTECTION FROM
UNLAWFUL SEARCH AND SEIZURE

all people are protected from all unlawful searches and seizures lacking a warrant clearly identifying whom and what is to be searched.

On one occasion in 1987 the security police came looking for me because of a drawing that I'd published.

JONATHAN SHAPIRO

The modern world we live in is vibrant and well connected. It seems like, more than ever before in human history, we all know people from different places. With the advents of social networking, smart phones, and the Internet, we can now share ideas and stay in touch more and easier than ever, yet because of all these wonderful inventions, many think we are now not entitled to have our lives be our own. All the people I know have parts of their lives that they share with others and other parts that they keep to themselves. Sadly, there are many people out there who think we are not entitled to keep those parts to ourselves and will go so far as to walk right in without cause or reason and take them from us.

The centers of most of our worlds are our homes. I know I consider my home my sanctuary from the outside world. It is where I go to truly be myself, relax, create, enjoy, entertain, and think. Yes, I did use the word *sanctuary*—because that is the way I see it. After long days of dealing with the outside world, the best thing for me to do is to walk through the door of my home; it feels like I am being welcomed by an old friend with a warm hug. Whether one's home is a house in the suburbs, a mobile home, or a hut—whatever and wherever that sanctuary is, it is his or her own to do with as he or she pleases.

As wonderful as my sanctuary and everyone else's may be, there are others who do not see it that way. There are people who feel they can barge in on our lives and use false statements and weak excuses to search and rummage through our lives and sanctuaries, many times imprisoning or destroying people in the process. Thousands in our world daily have that very thing done to them. Most times it is because they are accused of being anti-establishment, terrorists, or just nasty people. I am not denying that some people aren't, in fact, these things, but there are those who feel that, because they have power, they can do whatever they like to those they govern.

Most people want to live their lives and go about their days without causing problems for or harm to themselves or others. However, among those in power, some feel they can intrude upon our lives because they feel threatened by how we think differently than they do or because they feel insecure about their own lives and power bases.

If someone comes into my home without invitation, they had better have good reason and the legal right to do so and should not be doing it just because they think they can. I will openly admit that if someone did come into my home without the legal right to do so, they would find themselves at the wrong end of my lawyer's wrath. Sadly, there are many places where people could not fight back, places where governing officials can walk into someone's home without any legal grounds and the people thusly invaded would have no rights or recourse. Many governments see certain people as threats for one reason or another and, on the basis of these beliefs, perform illegal searches and take whatever they want from people's homes, ruining lives in the process.

One place where illegal searches are very common is in military concerns, places where rights are often set aside in favor of fighting, violence, and unnecessary hatred. History has shown us countless examples of this, from World War II to Vietnam to the frequent conflicts in the Middle East. Many of the stories around these war zone invasions sound strikingly similar - someone that showed support for one side has their home invaded by the other side. Often times arrests, destruction of privacy property, and even death can follow these horrendous acts.

In the modern world, many of us keep our dearest and most cherished secrets in our technological toys, from our home computers to our smart phones. Our techno lifelines are in many ways just as important and just as precious as our homes. The sad part is that the immortal hackers, as we call them, are just as guilty of invading our worlds and taking what they want as any dictator or power-hungry government figure is. I consider hacking and computer invasion to be in the same realm as home invasion and illegal search and seizure. Our technology is ours and ours alone. We all use security measures to do our best to keep our electronic lives safe, but many feel this part of our lives does not deserve to be protected and so they intrude upon them.

Our electronic toys are extensions of our lives and who we are as people. They are very similar to the diaries we keep and the secrets we stash away in the backs of our closets. Every person deserves to be allowed to keep to him or herself a special and sacred part of his or her life. No matter what any person or regime may say or believe, no one has the right to intrude on the inner sanctums of our lives without rightful and lawful cause to do so.

If the law determines that someone does have the right to search parts of our private world, he or she must secure the proper warrants to do so. The warrants should spell out what and where should be searched. Police and authorities should have to follow the same rules that all other people do. Many authorities and officials believe they are above the laws they enforce and can do as they please. As an old saying goes, lead by example.

Police should not be suggesting to "do as they say, not as they do." By treating people with decency and respect—not like things to be walked on and destroyed as one sees fits—we can all form societies built upon equal trust and dignity, not greed, intimidation, bullying, disrespect, and hate.

11 - FREEDOM FROM CRUEL AND UNLAWFUL IMPRISONMENT

no person shall be imprisoned without trial. No person shall be subject to cruel or unusual punishments. No person shall suffer injury while under arrest or imprisoned.

People should not be imprisoned without having the ability to challenge the legality of that imprisonment.

EFF BINGAMAN

For any society to survive and thrive, many things must be in place, but two of the most important would have to be justice and equality. True justice comes from many places in society, but most importantly from a legal system based upon truth and fairness. Justice is also a part of the punishments this system dishes out to those who violate the law and the rights of others.

"Let the punishment fit the crime" is a saying that has been around for many years, but it is still very relevant. If people commit real crimes, let them stand before their peers and a judge, answer for the crimes they have committed, and serve fair sentences that fit those crimes. We live in a civilized society, not a world of Neanderthals, so let us have a mature system of crime and justice.

To better understand why I included this freedom in this book, let's further discuss the devices and tortures employed by leaders and rulers. Strangely enough, as I was writing this chapter, I stumbled upon an article published by The Register, a UK based website that focuses on technology, in November of 2011 about how if you "like" a Facebook page that says something negative about the royal family of Thailand, you could end up getting fifteen years in prison. In the stories days gone by, we hear of kings and queens saying stuff like "off with their heads" for saying something the monarchy found not to their liking.

History provides a long list of people in power who dealt bizarre and cruel punishments for their own delight and personal gain or because they were scared of losing their power or being seen in a bad light. This list includes Hitler, Stalin, Attila the Hun, Maximilien Robespierre, Ruhollah Khomeini, Idi Amin Dada, Leopold II of Belgium, Pol Pot, Vlad Tepes, Ivan IV of Russia, Genghis Khan, Nero, and Caligula.

The tortures that these and other rulers dished out are so numerous and creative that it almost boggles the mind. I know many reading this section will even question whether or not these really happened, but there is documented proof for all of these. Some of the older methods of torture were written about or had sketches made of them, and some of the devices used still exist today and can even be found in museums around the world. For many of the events that happened in modern times, witnesses and victims are still around to tell of the horrific atrocities and cruelty they endured.

One of the more commonly known cruel punishments that many of us have heard of is crucifixion. This punishment is as horrific in real life as it has been made out to be by movies and pop culture. Another one that is widely practiced in some countries to this day is the amputation of body parts. In many countries, thieves will have their hands cut off. I saw a real video of this being done on the Internet—it was not Hollywood magic, and watching it made me physically ill. Even the Taliban has a history of using this form of torture and doing so in large public spectacles.

In medieval times, many forms of torture were used. If I were to name but a few of these forms I would be bound to include such horrendous acts like boiling alive, flogging, flaying, the breaking of bones, impalement, crushing, burning alive, sawing, slow slicing ("death of a thousand cuts" is a better name), the rack, the iron maiden, the Judas cradle, coffin torture, the knee splitter, the heretic's fork, the thumbscrew, and water torture.

The rack is one of the more well known of the lot. Victims would be strapped down and then they would be pulled apart at the seams. The poor souls would be ripped apart at their joints, making for a painful torture. The saw was another popular form of torture when the victim would be hung upside down and then basically cut in half. The Judas cradle was simply a pyramid shaped device that the poor soul was forced upon with the point being inserted into their vagina or anus. Most of the punishments inflicted were very creative ways to destroy a person and extract truth. I wonder how much truth came from a person being tortured and willing to say anything to stop the brutality.

One form of torture that has been used many times, even recently, is the hot box. I was first exposed to this form of punishment after watching a movie in which a prisoner in some corrupt Southern prison was locked in a steel box outside for several days. This form goes by many names and can involve different items, but the form of torture is always the same: the victim is locked in a box or container and left out in the elements to suffer. Sometimes it was only for a short span of time, but other times it was until death. The victim would be exposed to all the elements, from the heat to the cold to bugs to whatever else Mother Nature had in store. This form of torture has even been linked to the methods used at Guantanamo Bay.

Many prisons around the world, furthermore, have used this as a form of punishment, and some continue to do so to this day. There are even worse ones on record. There are reports that guards will mess with inmates time clocks and change their perception of day and night. Prisons have even been known to use music as a torture. In 1998, the Supreme Court of Israel went so far as to vote against a ban on loud music as an interrogation technique. They are not the only ones, it is reports that the USA has used this technique on several occasions. The most notable of these is on detainees in Iraq and Guantanamo Bay.

The location in which many of these tortures take place is the infamous dungeon. Even if we have never seen one, all of us have probably heard of it, and just its name instills some fear in us and activates our imaginations, which are fueled by history and Hollywood. Dungeons throughout the world and throughout history have been the main (but certainly not the only) locations where these barbaric and cruel acts have taken place. Many times, public spectacles are made of torture events. Public squares and gathering places are popular locations for these events. There are even reports from first hand witnesses that the Taliban used sport stadiums in cities such as Kabul and Kandahar as public forums for executions and amputations of criminals.

If we as a people are going to rise to our full potential, we confront all the aspects of our lives and the world, including crime and the punishments for committing crime. We need to dish out humane and just punishments that better reflect decency and fairness, not those of angry villagers, vengeful relatives, or evil, power-hungry sadists.

One type of punishment that leaves me with a heavy heart is capital punishment. If I am going to talk about punishments for crimes, this is really one kind of punishment I cannot leave out. It is a topic that is widely debated, perhaps more than any other aspect of crime and punishment. On the one hand, I do not believe in murder at all, but on the other hand, I do recognize the fact that some crimes are so severe and the perpetrators of those crimes so awful that capital punishment is the only recourse. What I do not believe in, though, is making such punishments cruel. Years ago I watched one of the *Faces of Death* movies (these movies showed many variations of death and even glorified them to some extent), and in this particular one they showed a real electrocution. It made me sick to my stomach to watch, and it also left a lasting impression on me.

If we are going to have capital punishment as part of our criminal justice system, we need to make sure it is not a cruel form of punishment. In the end, it is not what the criminal did but what we do that determines how we are judged. We should make sure the methods we use to carry out capital punishment are humane and just. From the research I have done so far, the most humane form I have been able to find is lethal injection. Why don't we think outside the box on this for a bit on this topic? Let's allow death row inmates to become organ donors. Using the most advanced form of lethal injection called the "one drug", the most humane form of capitol punishment to date that also will for the organs to still be safely be donated and help some of the many people that are currently sitting on waiting list.

When it comes to capitol punishment, I have the same outlook as I do in the rest of my life - let us take a bad and find some way to make a good from it. What if the bodies of those that have committed horrendous crimes be used to help others? I am talking about organ harvesting of death row inmates. The entire procedure could and would have to be done humanely and in the sterile environment of an operating room: no blood, no gore, just a safe and sane medical procedure to deal with the worst that go through our criminal justice system.

I am not a hypocrite and never will be. I do not believe that murder is right for any reason, but if capitol punishment is to be a part of our society then let us all find some way to make some good come of it. I actually think getting the capitol punishment for committing a serious crime is a hell of a lot easier to deal with then spending the rest of your life locked a way in a cell. Never having any freedom. You have someone telling you when to wake, sleep eat, exercise, subject to random searches, and told what to wear. Spending the rest of your natural life being reminded of the mistakes you made that got you to that point.

No matter how many laws we have, crime will still happen, but how we handle those that violate the rights of others is what is important. Do we want history to remember those who dish out punishments as cruel and heartless bastards or as wise and compassionate people? We need to make sure we have leaders and governing officials in place who know what true justice and who can dish it our fairly.

12 - BAN ON HUMAN SLAVERY
AND FORCED SERVITUDE

it is unlawful to forcibly hold, enslave, or imprison any persons against their will. It is also illegal to buy, sell, or exchange any person as a commodity.

Death is better than slavery.

HARRIET ANN JACOBS

Growing up in Louisiana, I learned about slavery and its social impact at an early age because of Louisiana's pre–Civil War history as a slave state. Even though that is now almost 150 years behind us, the impact of those times and events have left a lasting impact on the life, history, and social culture of the region. The Civil War was a ferocious war that lasted four years, cost many hundreds of thousands their lives, and tore apart a nation. Even though slavery officially ended in 1865 in the United States, there are still some rippling effects lasting even through to the current era from the war that was fought over slavery and the fight for rights that followed.

While researching for this section, I wanted to know more about slavery in our own times. Trust me: it only takes a few seconds to find out how much of a staggering problem it still is. Worldwide, we see it rear its ugly head to the tune of over twenty-seven million souls. That is over twenty-seven million of humanity's children being deprived of their rights, the same ones we enjoy.

Slavery is a very crafty and creative beast that has many faces. Two of the most common (but not by any means the only) forms of slavery found in our modern world are financial and sexual slavery. Quite often, ruthless business people will use the promises of good jobs, money, success, and even schooling to lure people into the trap of hopelessness that is slavery. Some people are what are called generational slaves, that is, slaves born into families that are slaves themselves. Some will go so far as to kidnap people into slavery. In war, captured people are enslaved like trophies.

Every corner of this planet has slavery in one form or another. I think the only continent that does not have slavery is Antarctica, which is also the only continent that does not have a permanent human presence. One of the places with the most infamous and longest history of slavery is Africa. Many of us in the Western world know of its history of shipping slaves like exports to Europe and colonies throughout the world. Most think that this died out ages ago and is now a thing of the past, but that is far from the truth. The slavery industry in Africa thrives even to this very day. The main areas affected now are western and central Africa. It is estimated that every year over two hundred thousand kids are forced into slavery. In some areas it is considered a traditional right to own chattel slaves (slaves considered personal property), especially among Arabs in Sudan and other regions of Africa. They treat their slaves as nothing more than things to be owned and used. They often work them as servants and concubines.

It is not just kids being forced into slavery, though: it is also grown men and women. Some are seen as simply the spoils of war, and others just happened to be in the wrong place at the wrong time. A common theme of slave ownership now and in years past is the destruction of the culture and religion of slaves. Many times slave owners force their slaves to take their own religion, even using force and torture to do so. There are documented cases of Arab slave owners forcing their slaves to become Muslims or having to pay a heavy price.

The other most common form of slavery, sexual slavery, is when either young women or young men are forced to become prostitutes. They are forced to have sex with "johns," whether they like it or not. They are not allowed their freedom and have no control over their lives. Younger girls are often in highest demand and are worked until they are no longer profitable for their owners. Unwanted pregnancies and forced abortions are a part of life in the sexual slavery world. If the prostitutes do get out from under the strong arm of slavery, they often cannot go home and have trouble getting help or work because of the stigma of being a sex worker, even if it had been by force.

One area of the world that has earned an infamous reputation for its sex industry is Asia, especially Thailand. Every year, thousands upon thousands travel there for a bit of vacation fun. The hidden side of this fun is the cost in human souls. While many of the sex workers work willingly, there is still a very high number that are not. Thousands every year are tricked, sold, forced, or manipulated into it. In the world of slavery, lies are so commonplace that many slavers and their henchmen could not tell the truth to save their backsides.

Many times kids end up in this world because their parents either outright sell them or are tricked by the promise that their children are going to be working or going to school and getting a good education. Sometimes the parents will even be given an advance on a child's earnings. That goes a long way in impoverished communities. It not only makes things look good to the parents, giving them some sort of peace of mind, but it also makes it easier for the slavers to get more from the same area. You know how it goes and what the other parents are thinking: "Well, if it is good enough for them, it is good enough for us." All of it puts a new twist on the old saying "keeping up with the Joneses." Sadly, there are even reports of some parents willingly selling a child into slavery to improve their lives financially, even if it only allows them to buy a few new things.

China and India are the two largest countries by population. In fact, about one-quarter of the world's entire population can be found in these two countries. That leads to many problems, including slavery and forced servitude. In India, a commonly known form of slavery is called "carpet slavery," which involves children and even adults being forced to work weaving carpets for many hours and then sleep near their looms. These slaves are often badly treated, live in poor and unsanitary conditions, and are treated like throwaway commodities. Once most slaves have outlived their usefulness to their owners, they are sold off or worse.

In China, many forms of slavery are encouraged by corrupt government officials and greedy businessmen. If you go to prison in China, expect to perform slave labor in one of the country's factories (they're sometimes referred to euphemistically as reeducation camps). Abductions right off the street are commonplace and even increasing in this corner of the world, too, to meet the needs of a global economy that demands huge amounts of cheap goods. Even children are not safe from this nightmare.

Next on our slavery world tour is Europe, where striving to make a better life can lead to an enslaved one. We have often heard this very common story: someone hears of a job in a far-off place with great pay and is even offered transportation to get there, only to eventually find out he or she has been played and ends up a slave. Many women fall into this trap and end up being forced into prostitution and servitude. Many criminal gangs and mafias make huge money by trafficking people and from the forced labor of their slaves.

People tricked into slavery are removed from familiar surroundings and kept under close watch, if not bondage. They are threatened and often beaten. Rape and sexual assault are very common in the world of slavery. It is even being reported that criminal gangs are going so far as to prey on and enslave homeless people. Criminal gangs that do get caught enslaving people usually lie and say they were actually helping the people they enslaved. Slavers will find ways to get slaves arrested and brought up on false charges. Some slavers will even kill slaves and dispose of their bodies without any remorse.

Our next stop is the good ol' USA. Most people think slavery in the United States ended in 1865 with the end of the Civil War, but that is far from the truth. It is estimated that over 250,000 people are currently enslaved in this country under various forms of slavery. Most are working in the sex industry, but slaves can also be found working as domestics, nannies, factory workers, and field hands. They can be found anywhere that greed overrides any sense of common decency. Slavers and slave owners will tell stories of how they are helping the enslaved and can even convince themselves of this while they force them to work for little or no pay, strip them of their freedom, and even remove them from all contact their families. The US government, like many governments around the world, strives to try to end slavery and human trafficking through many laws and acts, one of the most recent being the Trafficking Victims Protection Act of 2000. One of the many things this act does besides broadening the scope and definition of slavery is that it also guarantees the enslaved will be protected from deportation so long as they testify against their captors and enslavers. That is a nice and pretty start, but we need to go further than that. There are hundreds of thousands across the United States who would agree.

The story of slavery and trafficking in the Americas only begins with the United States, as almost every other country is also affected by this horrific plague. In Haiti, over one hundred thousand kids have been sold by their parents into slavery in order to try to earn a better life for their children and themselves. Most of the children are sold to rich families as domestic help, but oftentimes their servitude can also include sexual and physical abuse.

South America, a continent with a long history of slavery, still battles with it to this day. As with many places around the world, people are lured there with the false promises of good jobs and other benefits to their lives. Due to its large undeveloped areas and the far distances between many towns and ranches, makes it the ideal place for slavery to grow and prosper. Many ranch and business owners are often above the law and have no fear of what little will happen to them if they are discovered. There are reports that few, if any, slave owners have ever served jail time for their actions, though some have had to pay small fines. They consider these fines the small costs of doing business.

Globally, hundreds of businesses use and profit from slave labor, and many of us buy the products made by them. The number of slaves increases annually due to the global demand for cheaper and cheaper goods. Many of the businesses lie and deny and find unique ways to hide the facts and skirt around the truth. The slaves producing the goods we consume make little or no money and oftentimes work in horrendous conditions with little regard for safety. Every so often, the news media sensationalizes the fact that someone or a company is using slave labor. That is all fine and good, but let's be real and openly name and shame all the companies and people using slave labor to make and manufacture goods, not just whoever is going to draw the biggest headlines.

According to reports, there are at least fifty-eight countries globally producing goods by means of slave labor. The goods they produce cover just about everything, including clothing, fireworks, electronics, jewelry, food, footwear, household items, and more. Even the Christmas decorations you put on your Christmas tree could be the product of slave labor. That leaves a warm feeling in your heart, doesn't it? While you're celebrating, others are struggling for survival. If you want to know more about the full extent of goods being produced by slavery, I highly advise you check out the website <u>productsofslavery.org</u>. This website is supported by Anti-Slavery International, one of the largest organizations fighting the battle against slavery in the modern world.

If humanity and all of its children are going to prosper and thrive, we need to respect and encourage everyone who walks the face of the Earth, not just those who we deem worthy. Some of humanity's future leaders, saviors, and champions could be some of the very people that are held in bondage and slavery. We all need to take greater responsibility for our actions and not just sit by and make excuses while supporting evil and doing our part to further defile the value of a human life.

13 - RIGHT TO VOTE

all persons over the age of eighteen are entitled to the right to vote. No person shall be persecuted, fined, threatened, jailed, beaten, killed, or taxed for doing so.

A vote is like a rifle; its usefulness depends upon the character of the user.

THEODORE ROOSEVELT

All of the rights in Humanity's Bill of Rights depend on our having the freedom of choice, and that includes being able to choose those who lead and govern us. By choosing our leaders, we also choose the paths that our lives, cultures, and societies take. In order for the choices we make to be valid, however, all people who are affected by the leaders we choose must be able to vote. Voting should not be restricted to those of a certain gender, color, race, or social class or limited for any other reason. I do believe the only limiting factor should be age, with eighteen being the minimum age for voting. Most countries in the world recognize an eighteen year old as being mature and responsible enough to make an independent and informed decision for themselves. As of writing this most countries in the world have 18 as the minimum age for voting.

A true leader must represent all people, not just some. For many years, humanity has found ways to discriminate against people by restricting who could vote. Woman and minority groups, especially, have been discriminated against in this manner throughout history and even in the modern era. In some cases, only landowners are allowed to vote, but it is easy to see how unfair this can be: they will elect officials who will side with them and their own politics.

Nowadays, many countries, like the United States, take a laissez-faire approach to voting. They give people the right to vote but often couldn't care less if they do not. In Australia, a much different approach has been taken to voting: voting is considered a civic duty, and all citizens of at least eighteen years of age are required by law to vote. Failure to do so will result in a fine of at least twenty dollars but as much as fifty if one fails to rectify the situation. I am not the first to say the Australian voting system nonetheless leaves a lot to be desired, but the commitment to encouraging voting is very admirable. This is an approach that should be replicated around the world. Instead of limiting who can cast votes, make it every person's duty to vote. Ensuring all the people who can vote will vote is the only sure way to ensure the governing bodies are truly representing the people.

Giving people the right to vote is only one side of the equation; it is also very important to make it easy for people to reach polling places and be able to cast their votes as well as to ensure the system in place for registering people to vote is fair, unbiased, and also up-to-date. France is one of the most progressive countries on this front, because when someone turns eighteen, he or she is automatically enrolled to vote. It has also been reported that Norway has set up a very efficient system of voter registration as well, where the voter registers are automatically updated because they are also the tax lists as well as the lists for receiving national health care. Not only are these countries making it easier for people to be enrolled to vote with these systems, but they are also decreasing the amount of bureaucracy of their respective governments and saving their people millions of dollars every year by doing so.

All people casting votes must be allowed to do so without facing any repercussions for their choices. I do believe that what is called block voting or "village voting" must be abolished. This refers to the custom present in some cultures of the world that allows the head of a village to cast the votes for all the people he or she governs. If a villager opposes the choice and states his or her opposition, he or she can face persecution or banishment. What is even worse is, when someone running for office is afraid of losing, they will attack the groups of people who they feel will offer the greatest resistance. Both of these kinds of things occur often in many areas of Africa.

It is important for Humanity's Bill of Rights to work that we have the proper leadership to help bring humanity into the future. The leadership needed to accomplish this is going to have to consist of true leaders who really represent all of the people, not just the privileged ones. Those who choose to run for office must do so with the understanding that to serve in a public office means to serve the people and to be willing to listen to their voices and their votes and to respect their decisions , rather than to be motivated by greed and power—to do anything less is to disrespect oneself, the voters, and humanity.

14 - FREEDOM FROM VIOLENCE

no person shall be subject to any form of violence, whether it is from another person, government, or military group. This includes physical violence against one's person as well as sexual violence. Furthermore, no person shall ever be subject to war or the use of war implements against him or her in any way, shape, or form.

The pursuit of truth does not permit violence on one's opponent.

MOHANDAS GANDHI

It does not take much looking around to realize that violence is one of the forces most destructive of humanity. Every day around the world, thousands are killed by some form of violence, whether it's war, crime, assault, rape, torture, or bullying. It does not take much to recognize why we need this freedom to be included in Humanity's Bill of Rights and why every person on this planet needs to be assured that violence should not be a part of their life.

In the last one hundred years, it is estimated that at least one hundred million people around the world have lost their lives to war and conflict. In that time, we have seen humanity's capability for violence increase with the advent of some of the most destructive weapons imaginable as well as crueler methods of killing and injuring others. Wars serve no good, only murdering people, destroying lives, ruining cities, wasting valuable resources, and boosting the egos of warmongers who can't see past their own greed and selfishness.

My own family's past when it comes to war and violence has left a big impression on my life. In December 1969, one of my father's brothers was killed in that horrendous conflict called the Vietnam War. Almost exactly one year later, another brother was found dead under suspicious circumstances. His death was labeled a suicide, but everyone in the family believes beyond a shadow of a doubt that it was a murder. The scars from those two violent deaths dealt to our family in a short amount of time have remained with us to this day—over forty years later.

My family is not the only one like this in the world, sadly. Every day, thousands more families join mine as ones that have been affected and scarred by the tragedies of violence. It saddens me to think of how many families are being robbed of their loved ones for no good reason. How many families have been touched by the evil of violence? Violence is quite powerful in the sense that it can sometimes not only affect the person it is happening to but can also impact the people associated with them and even trickle down to future generations. I do not care what anyone else has to say about it: that is unfair to everybody.

Violence is also a powerful force in that it can take on many shapes and forms but always leads to the same thing—destruction. Most of the violence we face in this world is not on the mega scale of war but is more personal. Rape, assault, murder, bullying, kidnapping, humiliation, degradation, and theft are just some of the many forms of personal violence we all face in this world. No one deserves to be a victim of violence and to have its evil tentacles in his or her life.

One of the ultimate forms of violence that humanity has let loose upon itself is the nuclear weapon. We have already seen the power, devastation, and loss that can come from the use of nuclear weapons of war. We also already know that nothing good can come from using these weapons, yet humanity still insists on creating them as a means to an end—but what end? They are a quick fix, an easy solution for a problem that is too complex to just be solved by a bomb. There are so many of these weapons in the world now that we could use them to easily destroy ourselves and every other form of life on this planet many times over. Why?

Why do we need these weapons? If we listen to our leaders they will have us believe that we need them around for the times when our politicians want to play a game of who has the bigger dick. All I can say is that this is a game humanity no longer needs nor can afford to play because it does not do anyone any good when it's played; in the end, we all lose, every last one of us.

Violence doesn't take place on just the battlefield or in back alleys. One place where they have become increasingly prevalent is in sporting events. In talking with friends about violence and sports, one topic that came up many times was spectator violence at sporting events. Often it seems that the greatest violence happening at sporting events is not to the participants but to those watching it. It is quite common, it seems, for people to get so wrapped up in an event that they start abusing and assaulting each other; they think it is OK because it is at a sporting event, but it is not OK. Ask anyone who has seen the violence of a soccer riot firsthand or watched parents go bonkers at a children's sporting event about it to discover what it is truly like. If we are going to have sporting events, we need to put our own violence aside—we need to avoid making an unwilling spectator or event worker the recipient of unwanted violence—and leave it to the professionals who enter into the sport willingly.

Another form of violence I will go on the record for speaking out against is domestic violence. Every day around the world, millions of people suffer needlessly at the hands of those they love. Someone who is close to me and an important person in my life is a victim of domestic violence to this day. I will not name this woman, but I will speak about the hell she deals with. Most of the violence is not physical (although some of it is) but verbal. This woman has endured this crap for so long that she has been beaten down, and it is only because of the efforts of those around her who love her that she is slowly regrowing her backbone and learning to stand up for herself.

Even her children have suffered abuse at the hands of this man. He once pulled a gun on one of their sons, and the family got the police involved. What kind of man does something like that to his own flesh and blood? I have trouble calling anyone like that a man; I would consider him a mindless, immature jackass. To this day, their daughter is scared of her father and will make every effort to avoid being around him. That is no way for anyone to live, and it does not benefit anyone. It instead destroys people and ruins great potential. Truthfully, the only reason I am not naming this woman is to protect her from the harm he may inflict upon her for my writing. This is a story that gets repeated many times over every day around the world, and it needs to stop.

Every minute of everyday, somewhere in our world, someone is ridiculed, bullied, and humiliated because there is something about him or her that someone else does not like. The list of reasons why is longer than any other around, but the consequences are all the same: someone has some form of violence thrust upon him or her. Many times blood is never drawn, but the scars of violence are still there . The scars of violence are scars that we can carry with us and be affected by throughout our lives, even if the events that left such scars were but small moments in time. The scars can even carry themselves beyond and affect future generations.

Some have argued that some of humanity's greatest innovations come from the result of wars that have been fought, but at what price? How many lives are destroyed and ruined for that progress? I have even heard it said by some that war is necessary—bullshit. War and violence happen because at least one person, instead of doing what is right for all of humanity's children, does not give a shit about more than just themselves and their own self-serving interests. Humanity as a whole as well as individuals on their own need to ensure that they can grow, thrive, and prosper, but that is hard to do if we as a species are more determined to destroy and violate each other than to guard and protect each other.

15 - BAN ON CASTE SOCIETIES

all people shall live in societies without caste systems and societies that do not put limits upon a person because of his or her social status. All people shall be entitled to all rights equally.

All men are created equal; it is only men themselves who place themselves above equality.

DAVID ALLAN COE

Equality, fairness, and respect form the basis of Humanity's Bill of Rights. In order to fully achieve these things, we must ensure that all people are treated the same. Sadly, in our world at present, many cultures and societies think it is OK to treat some people differently. In some cases it is due to people's religions, backgrounds, or skin tones. In some it is even worse, and social status is generational.

It was not a very long time ago in the United States when nonwhite people were treated as second-class citizens. It was a time when rights depended on the color of your skin, and if you happened to be a different color, it would determine where you could go to school, where you could go in public, and even where you could sit on a bus. Many of the negative attitudes developed from this period of time have even managed to trickle down to current generations and influence modern social attitudes.

According to Wikipedia, there are currently over 250 million people worldwide who are forced to live in multilevel or caste societies. Most of the countries with such societies are located throughout Asia and Africa. One of the most well-known countries in which this persists is India. India's caste system has been around for many years, and even in modern times, many people's lives are still affected by what caste they come from. Many people do not know this goes far beyond the borders of India, though. Other countries being affected by different versions of caste societies are Sri Lanka, North Korea, Nepal, Bangladesh, Nigeria, Cameroon, Gambia, Ivory Coast, and Sierra Leone to name a few.

Many argue that having social classes is an important part of their cultural identity; to me this sounds more like a sad excuse. If a culture's identity is one that is based upon segregation, labeling, and discrimination, I do believe there is something seriously flawed with the culture's overall approach and outlook. The level or caste you are born into can determine everything about your life, from where you can live and work to whom you can marry.

People who are forced to live in such societies face discrimination on many levels. In multilevel societies, people oftentimes look down upon the lower castes and even have badly conceived notions about others not on their level. Social mobility in caste societies is often unknown; people are typically forced to live lives thrust upon them rather than lives of their own choosing.

All one has to do is to look back on the pages of history to see the many people who came from the lowest ranks of society to rise up and make a difference in this world. One of the greatest such people who comes to mind is Oprah. She was born in a time when black people were looked upon as belonging to a lower class, and her coming from a poverty-stricken background was just another disadvantage socially. She worked her way up to become one of the most powerful and influential women in the world.

In return, she is using her social position and her resources to help better the lives of many others. Had she not been given the opportunity of social mobility, it would have not only greatly changed her own life but also the lives of the thousands throughout the world she has helped. She is but one of the many people out there in our world who are shining examples of the benefits of having a society that isn't class-based and allows for social mobility.

Humans are a social species. We all feel the need to talk and interact with others. Our ability to create social circles and use them to enhance our lives and better our surroundings is a natural part of who we have become, but the danger in this is to use our ability at creating social circles as a way of becoming elitist or excluding others is unacceptable and in the end we only end up hurting others and limiting ourselves. Throughout my life I have had the chance to meet and interact with people from every walk of life and feel that my life is richer for doing so. In modern times we have even take our social circles to the internet. Most of us have been exposed to people from other walks of life that we might not have otherwise met and in doing so have enriched our lives.

To rob people of the ability to decide their own future and where they want to be in life also means depriving a society of some of its greatest treasures. To restrict people in their lives instead of opening up doors to them also means restricting how much a society can grow. To deny people social mobility is to deny them their own evolution. One of the things that makes us so interesting is that we are a very social species, but we need to ensure that we do not use our ability to be social and to create social circles as a means of discriminating against others and of denying them chances that are rightfully theirs.

16 - A RULER'S TERMS OF POWER MUST BE DEFINED

no ruler shall be entitled to an unlimited term of power. All terms in office for lawmaking rulers must be defined and approved by the people being governed. The people also reserve the right to have a ruler removed from power if the ruler no longer serves the people or violates the rights of any of them. This does not apply to nonlawmaking figureheads of government.

Every dictator is an enemy of freedom, an opponent of law.

DEMOSTHENES

Throughout history, humanity has looked to its leaders for guidance, inspiration, and encouragement. Leaders light the way for the people they govern. In times of sorrow and distress, the first among those whom people look up to are the leaders they have chosen. People trust their leaders to make the right choices for them, and if the time comes when change is needed, it is the people's right to change their leaders.

Most times, change in leadership is accomplished peacefully through elections. Many countries go so far as to limit the number of terms a leader can spend in office. This is most evident in the United States, where presidents are limited to two terms of four years each. This has been in effect since the 1940s, when one US president was elected to four terms in office. In most countries, an election is seen as something very important. In the United States, elections for president are so popular in the public media that news coverage of them are shown worldwide and begins up to a year prior to the elections, but the same elections often have low voter turnouts of under fifty percent of the American voting population.

Without fair and equal elections for governing officials, the results are usually disastrous. One of the greatest examples of this is Russia. For many generations this country was ruled by czars, rulers who were usually out of touch with the peasants they ruled. After many years of poor leadership, the people launched the Russian Revolution of 1917. This revolution led to the establishment of the world's largest socialist empire and a long period of rule during which people had fewer rights than before.

Our modern world is loaded with examples of countries whose leaders feel they do not need to be elected. One of the most well-known would have to be China. China is one of the last few communist regimes left in the world. Although it is the world's largest exporter and many of us have loads of stuff in our homes with the "Made in China" stamp on them, it is still a single-party communist government that offers little in the realm of freedom to its people. In recent times the country has embraced capitalism and markets itself to other countries as the world's factory, but it is known to oppress its own people, allow slavery, and even make policies that endanger or kill the people.

One of the most extreme examples of leadership gone wrong would have to be North Korea. A country with a long history of disputes, North Korea is currently ruled with an iron fist by the most extreme forms of totalitarian governments history has ever witnessed. The present ruler of the nation, Kim Jong-un, recently inherited the job after the passing of his father, Kim Jong-il. The government works very hard to keep the country closed off from the outside world and doesn't think twice about dealing with people who oppose them in any way. The government has created massive prisons that are described by those that have seen them as some of the most inhumane conditions imagined. North Korea also has one of the largest percentages of its citizen making up its armed forces. North Korea has been known to attack others without provocation simply as a show of its strength.

The list of absolute monarchs, dictators, and totalitarian rulers throughout history is so long that it could take several books just to discuss them all, but I will touch upon several of history's more memorable rulers who were above being elected. The Egypt of ancient times was a land ruled by pharaohs, or "living gods on Earth," as they referred to themselves. We know of many of these from pop culture, including Amenhotep, Ramesses, Seti, Cleopatra, and Tutankhamun. They ruled the lands of Egypt for thousands of years. They held onto this belief that they were gods on Earth and ruled as such. They constructed enormous monuments that consumed much of their country's resources. They were even known to change the locations of their capitals on a whim, which required entire cities to be built and relocated to new sites. Their reign only came to an end with the rise of the Roman Empire.

Ancient Rome produced some of the most memorable self-serving rulers. We know much about ancient Rome, from the awesome monuments to the technological innovations, but we also know about how crazy some of the rulers were. One that tops the list is the emperor Caligula, who ruled from AD 37 to AD 41. While the first two years of his reign went very well and he did much to improve life for those he ruled, all that soon changed drastically. The last two years of his reign earned him his nickname "the mad emperor" because they were filled with sexual perversion and extravagances that emptied the coffers of the treasury. Ancient Rome is filled with such men who took power and ruled carelessly.

I do not even know where to start when tackling the monarchs of Europe through the ages. One that comes to mind right away was Henry VIII of England. He went so far as to start his own church just so he could rewrite the laws of marriage to suit him. The Catholic Church at the time of his reign had very strong views against divorce, but Henry VIII rewrote the book on religion in England, forcibly changing the Catholic country into a Protestant one without giving the people any choice on the matter just so he could go on to have six wives. He even had to deal with rebellions over the fact that he had taken away people's ability to worship as they chose. Had the people been given a choice, they would have been able to simply elect a new leader.

Another case that comes to mind in this realm comes to us from France, during the disastrous rule of Louis XVI. When he took the throne, he was not even twenty years old. He was highly unqualified to even attempt the job. Without proper knowledge and experience, he led a reign in France that was such a disaster that it led to a great revolution, his own execution, the end of a royal monarchy, and the world's introduction to the horrors of the guillotine. Had the people of France been allowed to choose their own leaders and make the choices that were right for them, all of this may have been avoided, but they were instead subject to the rule of an unqualified king who was more focused on enjoying his own luxuries in life than on tackling the hard issues that plagued his nation.

I am not trying to say that every elected leader will always make the right choice, but what I am saying is that a true leader listens to the voices of all the people and does the best under their power to guide them, to steer them from harm and into the arms of prosperity. It is for the people to choose who leads them, and we must always be reminded that "power is given, not taken." To be chosen as a leader in the ranks of humanity means to uphold the rights of all of humanity and its children. To ignore the rights of others to increase your own personal gains is one of the greatest sins a human can visit upon other humans. A wise person knows that the road to happiness is not paved with the blood of others.

17 - NO ONE CAN OWN THE SUN, WIND, RAIN, OR AIR

no person can lay claim to the rights of the sun, wind, rain, or air. It is also illegal to deny a person access to these things. Furthermore, it is also illegal to fine, tax, or otherwise penalize a person for collecting them. This includes (but is not limited to) requiring those who use naturally occurring energy resources such as solar or wind collection to pay higher rates.

Forests, lakes, and rivers, clouds and winds, stars and flowers, stupendous glaciers and crystal snowflakes—every form of animate or inanimate existence, leaves its impress upon the soul of man.

ORISON SWETT MARDEN

Since humanity's humble beginnings, a few things have always been there to help us during our struggles, growth, and prosperity. The Sun is the fuel for life on every corner of Earth, and with the rain, they help us to grow our crops and livelihoods. The wind has, for many generations, powered the sails of our ships as we have explored the world around us in wonder and excitement. Maybe more important than anything else, though, is one special thing, this thing that has been with us since the dawning of our species and will stay with us to the end of time: air. Air is that glorious mix of naturally occurring chemicals that gives us life. Without it we could not exist, and so it reminds us of whom and what we are.

Humans suffer for lack of the Sun; ever hear of vitamin D deficiency? Without the power that the Sun gives us, we simply would not be who we are, and we would not be able to survive. Without its light and warmth, we would not be able to grow our crops, raise our livestock, or build a bountiful life for ourselves. Everything about our species is a result of a caring relationship with the Sun. We are only just beginning to learn how to harvest the energy that it gives us for free. Even though solar panels have been around for some time, it is only now in recent years that we are better learning how to harness the power of the Sun and put it to use without causing any pollution or side effects.

Despite all it does for us, the wind gets the least respect out of all of the forces of nature. For many generations, sailors all over the world have relied on the wind's power to carry them across the globe. Looking back in our history books, we can see that almost all of the greatest discoveries throughout history have been able to happen because of the wind. From the time of the Vikings and of Columbus all the way to that of Captain Cook and beyond, even to our own modern era of global shipping, the wind has been there, although frequently silent. Since the dawn of time, the wind has been there to blow around our world the seeds that life needs to survive and thrive. The wind has also been there to carry the birds along in their flights.

In our modern era, we are even learning how to harvest the energy of the wind to fuel our lives. The city of Palm Springs in California is one place doing this. It is a city built from the desert, yet it has been turned into a luxurious oasis and paradise. At the heart of life in Palm Springs is the San Gorgonio Mountain Pass Wind Farm in the San Bernardino Mountains. It contains over four thousand wind turbines and generates enough power to fuel Palm Springs as well as the entire Coachella Valley. More and more regions and municipalities are looking to nontraditional sources of energy, including the Sun and the wind, to fuel their lives.

For countless millennia, the rain has also fueled life here on our planet. It is the reason why many cities were built where they are. Rains bring life to the crops and the trees we need to survive. Lack of rain has even been known to trigger events that have toppled governments and started revolutions. Throughout the world, even today, many homes, farms, and lives depend greatly on the rain that falls from the sky. Many countries and municipalities are even turning back to rainwater collection, or rain harvesting, as a means of easing strains on existing water supplies.

Australia, the most arid continent on earth, was faced with a decade of drought that saw many rivers and lakes dry up or greatly diminish in size. The country embraced rainwater collection, with the government even going so far as to offer rebates to help people pay for their rain tanks. It was due to these extensive measures taken by the government that the country was able to keep the water flowing and available to all people. In Utah, a different battle is being waged: rainwater collection is illegal. This was brought to the public's attention in 2010 when a business owner installed a rainwater collection system. It is also illegal in Washington and Colorado to gather rainwater, even if it falls on your own rooftop. In recent times, some progress has been made in these locales to change the laws.

Without air—glorious, fresh air—we would also not exist, plain and simple. We all learn from an early age that lack of air means death. Strangely enough, the idea that we should protect the air we breathe comes not from the news or from history but from science fiction. In the original version of the movie *Total Recall*, a group of people called "the mutants" who are fighting for their rights in a domed Mars colony had their area of the city sealed off and all of the air pumped out, which almost killed everyone in that section, good and bad alike. That part of the movie, though, had a strong effect on me. I cannot for the life of me ever see a reason to deprive anyone of the air he or she needs to breathe. Doing so is the same as putting a gun to his or her head and pulling the trigger; it is murder.

Both history and modern times give us countless reasons why these forces of nature need to be protected. We know that with all of these in place, humanity has a chance to thrive and prosper. When humanity takes its place among the stars and settles new worlds, we know these worlds will also have to have sunlight, rain, and air. Ensuring that all people have access to that which nature gives us freely not only ensures our survival but also helps safeguard our future.

18 - FREEDOM FROM POLLUTION

all people are entitled to live free of pollution and environmental contamination. All people and businesses should make it a high priority to clean up existing pollution and to prevent it from happening in the future.

The most important pathological effects of pollution are extremely delayed and indirect.

RENÉ DUBOS

Most members of humanity now enjoy the creature comforts our science and technology have made for us, but there is a price to be paid for our comforts and new way of life. The price is a high one that all members of humanity as well as many rivers and other animal species and even plants will have to pay—pollution. Hundreds of millions of people currently live in areas infested with pollution that is scientifically documented to have negative health effects on us as well as future generations.

Let's start with our cities, the centers of humanity's livelihood and culture. Our cities span the globe and take on every form imaginable, with skyscrapers and monuments of every kind of design. For all their glory and splendor, however, they have a darker side, and that is the pollution they generate. Industrial waste, human garbage, and air and water pollution are all parts of this. Most major cities on our planet suffer from these sins, and therefore so do the people who inhabit them. Even many of the homes we build to live in are now major sources of pollution.

Hundreds of millions of cars and trucks travel our roads and help to fuel our lives. They make much of our world possible to navigate, but despite offering this blessing, they are a double-edged sword. The dark side of this sword is that they spew endless amounts of toxins and pollutions into the air. As more and more cities grow, more cars and trucks come in to help fuel these expansions and the continued development, but almost every vehicle on our planet is fueled my fossil fuels. Fossil fuels are popular because they are cheaper than most other forms of fuel, but they are also well-documented sources of pollution. The exhaust from vehicles is responsible for countless illnesses, including asthma, lung and respiratory aliments, and shortened life span. Studies have indicated that air pollution is the cause of death of more than three million children annually, although the number may be much high than that—and that is also not taking any adults into account.

The industries that dot our cities provide us with almost everything, even many of the foods we consume. The pleasures, treasures, and joys that they bring to our lives, however, come at a very heavy price. The pollutants our industries generate are some of the worst on our planet. These tend to be worse in developing countries than in more modern, established countries due to regulations in place in the latter, but still it happens everywhere, and all of humanity suffers for it. We not only get to enjoy the fruits of our industries but also the air pollution, solid waste, and runoff in our waterways that comes with them. Many times those who live near factories and industrial sites suffer the worst of the pollution on offer, but they are not the only ones. Pollution from these sites can go downstream, seep into the ground, ruin groundwater supplies, and even take to the air. In one study, scientists were able to determine that pollution from China was able to make its way up across the Serbian tundra, across to Canada, and down to the west coast of the United States.

Much of the waste we produce to help improve our lives is not easily cleaned up or disposed of. When it comes to our household waste, much is buried or burned. The waste that is buried could take dozens or even hundreds of years to break down. The burned waste leaves behind toxins and chemicals that may take ages to dissipate. Radioactive waste produced from our power plants will take thousands of years to no longer be hazardous. For all of our science, very little of our waste is reused and made useful yet again.

Even the mines that are dug to supply the rare materials we need to create our delights can be some of the greatest sources of pollution. A case in point is the town of Pitcher, Oklahoma, which died by the very hand that created it. The town was centered on lead and zinc mines, and one by-product of the mining was toxic "chat" piles, the leftovers after the ore has been extracted. Even the groundwater was contaminated because of the poor practices that took place. Instead of setting up a safe and regulated site, they simply piled it up in mountains and the toxic chemicals were leached from the piles to help decimate the own and its people. The town has been abandoned now and will never be again, all thanks to the pollution humanity created. There are many more towns like this one that dot the globe, including Wittenoom in western Australia and Centralia in Pennsylvania.

Our rivers and waterways have been the lifeblood of humanity. Most of our major cities have been built along our watery treasures, and they have fed the flames of humanity's rise. The way humanity has treated them until now, however, has been appalling. Despite all they have given us, we have treated them like our dumping grounds. According to recent surveys, every major river in the world is considered to be in crisis. They are all dying for a wide range of reasons, but almost every reason comes back to actions taken by humanity. Humanity's greed and carelessness is now strangling the very lifeblood of so many cities.

It was only while researching this book that I learned a scary fact that affects me personally. I grew up along a tributary of the Atchafalaya River, and that river is now in trouble. I can still remember going down to the water to swim with my cousins, but now it is becoming too dangerous to do so because of the pollution from humanity's industries. I am not only talking about the local industries but also the ones upriver, many states away, where the waters that feed the river originate from. The river begins many hundreds of miles away, a half a country. Along that route are many homes, businesses, and industries whose lifelines are tied to the waters that eventually make their way down to the Atchafalaya River.

The Atchafalaya River is not the only river in dire straits. Most of the rivers in our world are in trouble. Our tales, legends, and stories tell us of all these amazing rivers, such as the Nile, the Amazon, the Mississippi, the Murray-Darling, the Mekong, the Rio Grande, the Danube, the Ganges, the Colorado, and the Yangtze, to name a few, but they are all now suffering horrific fates at the hands of humanity. The assaults and ailments they're suffering vary, but the end result is the same for all: death and disease to the river and to the life-forms (including humans) that inhabit these waterways and rely upon them.

Our rivers are not the only waterways in trouble. Lakes, seas, bays, harbors, and even oceans are in danger as well. One of the best examples of this damage can be found in the Pacific Ocean Garbage Patch, an area larger than the state of Texas floating out in the Pacific that is an accumulation of decades of garbage and human waste that keeps growing and does not break down. Experts believe the ingredients that make up the garbage patch could be around for thousands of years and that during that time, the waste will be continuously harmful to the life that calls that area of the ocean home and to the life that feeds upon it, which includes even humanity.

One of the most extreme examples of pollution in our waterways occurred in the Salton Sea in California. Originally, the Salton Sea was home to a growing and thriving resort community called Salton City, as well as other smaller communities along its shores. That all changed in the late sixties and early seventies when agricultural runoff started causing massive fish kills. One major side effect of this runoff is hydrogen sulfide gas. This gas was once used in World War I as a weapon, and now it is the harbinger of doom for so many that once lived at and enjoyed the Salton Sea. Experts have determined that the ecology of the Salton Sea may never recover from the toxins humanity has carelessly dumped into it and the resultant by-products of them, like hydrogen sulfide gas. To go to the Salton Sea now is to go into the heart of death and foul smells; it is no longer a trip to a seaside paradise.

It is not just the water we are poisoning and using to kill off our people and cities but also the very air we breathe. Humanity is addicted to its vehicles and relies heavily upon them for almost every aspect of life, yet the vehicles we have chosen spew forth tons of toxins every minute of the day. I really do find it hard to believe that for all of our advancements in science and research we have not been able to produce cars that do not rely upon burned biomass fuels. I stumbled upon an article about a so-called water-powered car designed by Genepax. I was able to discover that the company went belly-up before even getting off the ground, but an article published on treehugger.com takes an in-depth look at the technology behind this water-powered vehicle. The best their experts could figure out without having a vehicle on-hand on study was that the car really could not run on water but could use metal hydrides that work with the help of water to produce energy.

After reading all of this information, I contacted a good friend of mine who has a college background in science. She told me that it is theoretically possible to build a car designed to run on a metal hydride and water fuel system but that the main problem faced by this would be to make sure that the energy output is greater than the energy input. After having a very long talk with her about the many different characteristics of cars and fuel systems, I felt my mind blown by how we have so many avenues yet to explore that can offer us real and lasting fuel systems for transportation that do not pollute the environment. It is up to humanity to make its own choices and to further explore these routes, while avoiding becoming the victim of the many scams out there that are only chasing a buck and have no real science behind them or whose use would provide no benefit.

I even stumbled upon an article on the web saying Toyota was testing a vehicle that it wanted to be entered into the world record book as the fastest vehicle to run on compressed air. All I can say is, where is mine? I bet it would be better than the petrol-sucking beast I drive now. For decades, designers and creators have been dreaming up new and exciting ways for us to get around, and many of them could easily be made low-pollution or pollution-free. The website darkroastedblend.com even published an extensive article about retro future transportation. It was a fascinating article covering a wide range of concept vehicles by the thinkers of ages past predicting revolutionary forms of human mobility .

Some of the concepts were absurd, but many were not. They were exciting, fresh, and innovative, and they could hold the key to solving some of our pollution problems caused by our transportation. Some thought of taking the idea of a zeppelin airship to new heights and make them into the luxury liners of the skies. Another was the use of high speed trains, monorails, and suspended rail networks. Some even proposed a giant tube system for personal transportation. This idea was even a key form of transportation in the movie "Logan's Run".

Globally, there are many cities infested with pollution from a wide variety of sources, and millions are suffering and dying from the pollution we have caused. I was easily able to find a list of cities across the globe suffering from pollution. Some of them are New Delhi, India; Maputo, Mozambique; Niamey, Niger; Lomé, Togo; Moscow, Russia; Baghdad, Iraq; Mumbai, India; Mexico City, Mexico; Port-au-Prince, Haiti; Linfen, China; Mailuu-Suu, Kyrgyzstan; Norilsk, Russia; Sukinda, India; Dzerzhinsk, Russia; Chernobyl, Ukraine; and Kabwe, Zambia. I stumbled upon another tidbit of info while researching for this book: according to one report, the World Bank states that sixteen of the top twenty most polluted cities are Chinese. Even the home of the 2016 Summer Olympics, Rio de Janeiro, is suffering at the hands of pollution. I bet we won't be seeing any of the problems it's caused on TV when they are awarding those gold medals.

If we are going to continue to be a part of this world or any other, we need to take greater responsibility for our actions and deeds. Our self-centered views fueled by greed need to stop. We have the technology now to do many things and to do them safely. We can have all of our toys, innovations, and creature comforts, but we need to go about obtaining them in a manner that is not going to kill and murder other people as well as other species. When many hear this, the first words out of their mouths will be "but it will cost too much." Then, fine, how much are the millions of lives taken every year by our own stupidity, greed, and selfishness worth? Why doesn't someone grab a magic wand and bring back all of the species we have killed off and the ecosystems we have destroyed? Humanity has ravaged its home planet to the breaking point, and now its people are paying the price. If humanity is to survive, all of its people need to be able to live in an environment free of pollution. This environment must include not only our homes and cities but also the world around us. I know I enjoy having clean air to breathe.

19 - RIGHT TO THE BASICS OF LIFE

no person shall ever be denied access to food, air, water, and protection from the elements.

Never be bullied into silence. Never allow yourself to be made a victim. Accept no one's definition of your life; define yourself.

HARVEY FIERSTEIN

I once heard a saying that is so very true: "man cannot live by love alone." We all need several things in order to survive and thrive: food, water, air, shelter, clothing, the ability to earn a living, access to proper health care, and the same rights and privileges as those around us. For many of us, these are just natural, given parts of life, but many others, sadly, are greatly deprived of one or more of these. To be deprived of any of these means that one is unable to live their life to the fullest, and that not only means they will be losing out but also society as a whole.

People can be deprived of their basic rights for a variety of hard-to-control reasons—natural disasters, geographic phenomena, or lack of infrastructure, for example—but these are not the only reasons. Many people are deprived of their right to the basics of life because of the selfishness and cruelty of others who put their own desires above those around them. These people feel they are superior to others, and it is in fact quite common for many in power to use the basics of life as a bargaining tool to get others to do what they want.

There are many people in our world who think of the lives of others as things to be thrown away, as if they were disposable. These people can be found in every corner of our globe, from Africa to the Americas, from the most impoverished communities to the richest communities. These are people who do not see the value of a human life and cannot see why people deserve to have what it takes to survive. There are many still who think it is OK to beat people down and do whatever it takes to gain the upper hand over them. I believe that every person's life has value and merit.

This does not mean that everybody should have everything handed to them, but what I do believe is that we should give people access to what they need to survive. Many countries do recognize the fact that many people need some assistance in order to survive. In the United States, there is a food stamp program designed to help the impoverished buy food. During the recent financial crisis, that need was more apparent than ever when the number of Americans looking for help in putting food on their tables escalated to over forty-six million. Even the United Nations has a food program, called the World Food Program. This program feeds up to ninety million people every year, most of whom are children. Sadly, however, this is only a drop in the bucket, as a recent report from the United Nations states that over nine hundred million people worldwide are starving.

Water is also rapidly becoming a valuable commodity globally, as safe drinking water in many areas is becoming hard to find. Many water supplies have been heavily polluted. I once heard that future wars will not be fought over oil or riches but over water. I strongly believe this will be true if we do not turn things around and fast. We all need water to live and to help keep our bodies nourished, yet many are denied this basic of life. Sometimes it is due to geography and Mother Nature, yet sometimes it can be as a result of war, violence, greed, selfishness, and ignorance.

With all of our knowledge, wisdom, and technology, you would think that by now we would have figured out much smarter ways to use our water supplies and be able to make more of it available for others. In recent times, Australia was hit with a drought that lasted ten years. This saw many areas of the country get ravaged, but the government was wise enough to invest its money in a campaign to help conserve water and be more environmentally responsible. It is thanks to these efforts that Australia does have enough water for its people. Billions were invested to ensure there would be water to help fuel the people and also growth and prosperity.

Very few, if any, people live in an absolutely perfect environment where neither shelter nor clothing is needed. These are just the natural needs of any member of humanity; regardless of whether we are living in the most isolated outpost or village or in one of the large metropolises that dot our world, we all need clothing and shelter. Recent statistics estimate that over one hundred million people are homeless worldwide. I believe that may be a modest estimation.

The majority of the homeless worldwide are children, and they are also the most at risk and the most vulnerable. These children are the very future of our cities and nations. We will never know how many among them could have become great, whether they may have been brilliant writers and scientists or just parents raising happy and healthy families. These children end up homeless for a wide range of reasons, including war, violence, death, misfortune, slavery, and more. There are many organizations globally that are making efforts to change this and help those without. Tens of millions annually are helped by such organizations, but this is not enough.

If you look at the numbers and scale of things that we as humanity need to accomplish to ensure that all of us have this right, it might seem like a daunting task, but we can all do something. Simply by ensuring others have the rights included in Humanity's Bill of Rights, including the means to survive; we are opening doors for many who currently go without. By doing this we can better our own lives by increasing the richness and diversity of our world in which we all live.

20 - FREEDOM FROM ALL FORMS OF CENSORSHIP

no person shall ever be subject to any form of censorship, including but not limited to print, spoken, electronic, and artistic.

> *The only valid censorship of ideas is the right of people not to listen.*
>
> TOMMY SMOTHERS

When I was fourteen, an event took place that forever changed my outlook on life and how I saw things—the fall of the Berlin Wall. The world was celebrating the glorious day in November 1989 when that iconic symbol of communism and oppression fell. I knew this was important, but I knew very little. So I started reading and then kept on reading. I learned about people who were ravaged by war and then ruled by cruel heartlessness for decades after. The members of humanity locked behind these walls had no free voices, and their knowledge of the world came only through government-controlled media. To contradict the government was oftentimes a deadly move.

This culture these people lived in was a strange concept for me in my corner of the world. I had free access to books and information, the same things that so many had to fight for. It was around this time that I learned a hard fact I did not like: censorship was a part of the lives of billions worldwide, including my own. I spoke with one of our librarians about censorship, and she told me there was a banned books list for the library of the high school I was attending. I asked to see the list but was denied, so I do not know what titles were on it. That really made me angry because I felt I should be entitled to that knowledge.

Since I couldn't see that banned book list, I decided to do the next best thing and check out the current list of challenged books list published by the American Library Association. Many of the most objected books include many great literary works. We are talking about books by such well known authors as F. Scott Fitzgerald, Harper Lee, John Steinbeck, George Orwell, Ernest Hemingway, J.R.R. Tolkien, Upton Sinclair, and Jack London to name a few. Many of these writings, as well as others, bring different aspects of our world and humanity to our doorsteps and, by doing so, offer unique insights into our world and ourselves. Controversial classics like *Animal Farm* and *1984* warn us of what can happen if we let things get out of control and give up control of our lives to others. Heart warming hits like *The Color Purple* and *The Grapes of Wrath* show us what hardships, happiness, sorrow, and triumphs people can endure and overcome.

Here is a short list of books that have been banned: *The Adventures of Huckleberry Finn, The Catcher in the Rye, To Kill a Mockingbird, Bridge to Terabithia, Lord of the Flies, Of Mice and Men, The Color Purple,* the *Harry Potter* series, Anne Frank's *The Diary of a Young Girl, Arabian Nights, The Awakening, Brave New World, Call of the Wild, Fahrenheit 451* (a personal favorite), *The Grapes of Wrath, Gulliver's Travels, I Know Why the Caged Bird Sings, James and the Giant Peach, Lady Chatterley's Lover, Light in the Attic, The Scarlet Letter, Uncle Tom's Cabin, A Wrinkle in Time,* and the Bible.

Not very long ago, most of our fights to give ourselves a voice and eliminate censorship took place on the airwaves and in the realm of publishing.

Those battles are still taking place worldwide anywhere the voices of people and freedom are being silenced and restricted, but now the fight has grown to include the mightiest tools of them all: the personal computer and its offspring, the Internet. These electronically fueled gems allow for all members of humanity to broaden their horizons, create meaningful social networks, strengthen family bonds, and easily exchange ideas.

Never before in humanity's history have we ever been so well connected. Our toys and tools help us reach out to every corner of the globe as easily as walking down the block from our homes. We have such fun tools, like Facebook, Google, and Twitter, that make it so easy for each of us to be a part of so many different lives. Sadly, many in our world do not have the luxury of the freedom to explore and interact with others online because the powers that be believe people should not be allowed to think freely and openly explore the world around them. They are forced under the iron hand of oppression and made to live under the rule of those who deny them the rights to openly speak, learn, live, and love.

The Internet has been labeled by many as one of the greatest tools in the history of humanity, and many feel it is their right to have access to it. I agree and believe it should not be regulated by any government, but many countries do not feel that way. There is an ever-increasing number of countries controlling what the people in their countries can say, think, do, and see on the Net. The countries that have the most Internet censorship are Burma, China, Cuba, Iran, North Korea, Saudi Arabia, Syria, Turkmenistan, Uzbekistan, and Vietnam. These are the most controlled countries where you are limited in the sites you can visit and what you can say. Everything you do and say are monitored.

Another sixteen countries have been listed as "under surveillance." This refers to countries whose Internet is monitored and even has some sites blacked out. The argument for doing so is the same "protecting the people" rigmarole. In Australia, the country I currently call home, the Internet is filtered. Isn't *filtered* just a cute word? It makes it sound like coffee. The truth is that if information contrary to what higher powers gets out there, they want to be able to squash it. In July 2010, a journalist for

The Age newspaper said the government censored 90 percent of a meeting with ISPs and business leaders about censorship before releasing it to the media. Australian law allows full access to all government documents, yet the attorney-general's office said releasing an uncensored version could have set off "premature unnecessary debate." Unnecessary debate my ass. We are talking about the freedom of access to the Internet for an entire nation. People should have a right to know what their politicians are deciding on their behalf. The politicians just did not want to have to deal with a mess of their own making. Keeping secrets also makes it easier for those in power to stay in power and to fight against any force that threatens that power.

Even though internet censorship is a key topic in our present day media, it is not the only form out there. One of the most talked about realms and areas where censorship loves to rear its ugly head is in books and our printed documents. Many of the greatest books of our cultural history have been, at one time or another, banned. They have been banned for various reasons, the most common being because the writing offended someone and the powers that be were threatened by what was written. It was not hard to find lists of books on the Net of banned works; I have read many of them, and I am proud that I did. If you wish to find more books that have been banned, please check out the American Library Association or the extensive listing compiled by Wikipedia. It might just blow your mind to see some of the works of literature that have been banned. I must say that the books on the list I have read have made me laugh, cry, be angry, worry, wonder, think, imagine, and contemplate various aspects of my own life. I feel I am richer for reading those books along with all of the other books I have read. It will not surprise me to hear one day that this very book has been placed on a banned book list. It might make me sad and upset, but it will not surprise me.

Censorship inhibits the natural growth of humanity and its children. For us to grow, we need knowledge to learn from, and we need to be able to think openly and draw conclusions of our own designs. Every one of our advancements in this world and in our history has been because people have taken bold steps and thought outside the box, but if you limit what they can read, think, and do, you are stifling the natural creativity of life. I could be opening a Pandora's box by advocating for the abolishment of censorship, but in the end, I do believe people need to be free to make their own choices and decisions in this world. My mom always told me, "You need to do what is right for you, because only you know what will make you happy."

Each of us has our own road to travel in life. This road will at some point have each of us seeking answers to the questions we have. Once you start down that road, how far do you let it go? Under the cruel grip of censorship, people, ideas, writings, discoveries, and even inventions are silenced for a wide variety of reasons, most having to do with control, power, and enslavement. Censoring the information and knowledge available to members of humanity ultimately does more harm than good. I say this because to limit what a person can know is to limit how far we can progress and develop as a species. In years to come, humanity is going to face great challenges, and the very people who are being censored could hold keys to some of the answers we will need to survive. We must never forget one hard fact: knowledge is power.

21 - RIGHT TO EQUAL TAXATION

all people shall pay an equal percentage of taxes, with no person paying a lesser percentage than anyone else.

In this world nothing can be said to be certain, except death and taxes.

BENJAMIN FRANKLIN

The above quote is one I grew up hearing and still strongly believe holds true, but there is a darker reality to taxes. In our modern world, taxation is highly unfair, and most times it favors the rich and well connected over the average person. In most corners of the globe, the hardest hit with taxes are the ones who least can afford it. Our leaders the world over are always banging the "fair taxes" drum, but what usually happens is the same thing that always happens: the rich, the privileged, and special interest groups get tax cuts and special benefits, while the poor and the middle class are left to pick up the bill for everything.

One of the greatest complaints throughout history and in many societies has been that taxes are unfair, and we all know this is true. Let's put the bullshit and excuses aside. Taxation policy favors those with the money, influence, and power to change the minds of those with the abilities to change taxation policy. Before I get started, I will state this: any fair taxation does not stand a chance if people keep on granting special loopholes and clauses that benefit certain parties and friends of those in power.

The US tax system is the one most written about worldwide. It seems like every week we get to read about some battle raging in congress or the White House about tax hikes or tax cuts. Looking for facts online can be a bit rough, but the general consensus seems to be that the US tax code is at least a few million words long and grows annually. It is labeled as one of the most complex tax systems globally (Germany and India, however, have tax codes that are considered to be worse than that of the United States). If you look at the basic tax code layout, it looks all nice and fair, but that is in reality far from the truth. The US tax code is written for the rich and powerful, and its policies are dictated by them. There are so many loopholes and ways for the rich to make deductions. One of the most popular is using real estate and investments as ways of dodging and outright avoiding paying taxes.

We cannot leave out other countries in our talks about tax. While doing research for this chapter, it was very easy to find people from all over the world complaining about taxes. I have read comments from people from every corner of the globe, including people from Germany, India, Australia, and Canada to name a few, complaining about how unfair and how complex the tax systems in their countries are. Without fair taxation, many countries and regions breed discontent and bias among their people, and this can even lead to the sowing of the seeds of discontent.

If history has taught us anything, it is that if the people are not happy and satisfied, major changes in government and civil unrest could follow. Many governments around the world and throughout time have been uprooted because of the way they treated and thought of the peoples they were governing. One of the big contributing factors to the great French Revolution that led to the end of a monarchy was the ineffective way in which the French government of the day handled taxation. It took a common approach that many governments take: instead of cutting spending, it kept on taxing the people. That is an easy approach, but it is one that cannot be maintained because people can only be taxed so much.

Under most current tax systems around the world, the rich and powerful are the ones who benefit from the way the tax laws are written, leaving the poor and the working class to carry the largest burden of providing revenues from taxes. Many countries even use taxation as a way of keeping the poor down and exerting greater control over them while ensuring the powerful stay in power. One of the greatest challenges President Obama has faced during his term in office has been dealing with Congress and its rich boys club. Members of Congress have been so obsessed with protecting their rich friends and families and keeping the poor oppressed that they even strong-armed the president into approving more tax cuts for the rich by agreeing to continue Bush era tax breaks in exchange that would help the struggling people of a country on the brink of total economic collapse. I found out about this through an article from the UK based "The Guardian" in December 7, 2010. Instead of doing their part to try to help the people recover from a situation that they helped to create, members of Congress gave themselves tax cuts and then cut spending to programs that would have made a real difference.

The fairest way for taxation to happen and the method that will appeal to the most people is taxing everyone at the same rate, which is simply referred to as having a flat tax. It is a system that gives few if any special privileges in the form of deductions and exceptions. There has been much written about flat taxes in the last twenty years, with many people giving their two cents on the matter. One of the best books written on the topic to date is called *The Flat Tax*, by Robert E. Hall and Alvin Rabushka. in this book, the writers' have put forth a simple and effective plan to tax all income once and only once. This book's approach to flat taxation is definitely one that is based upon sound economic principles, and it avoids the pitfalls and loopholes that plague tax systems globally. The simple approach would also alleviate many extra costs for families such as accountants and tax lawyers.

Many believe the flat tax is a new idea, but it is far from it. It was first recorded in 1861, during the time of Abraham Lincoln. It fell out of favor due to pressure from the wealthy industrialists of the age. After that, it made a small resurgence in the early 1960s, but it did not catch on fully again until the early 1980s. From there it continued to gain ground in the public and political discourse until it hit the big time again in the 1990s. It is reported that at least twenty-five countries now have flat tax systems in place, with a few more currently considering it. These tax systems are some of the fairest of all—what you earn is what you pay tax on. Fair is fair; the percentage and tax cuts one person gets are the same as what the next person gets.

Another advantage of the flat tax is that it allows many people to handle their own tax affairs in a simple and easy manner. Many people no longer have to pay outrageous amounts of money to lawyers, accountants, and tax filers to do what they are able to do themselves. It also results in major financial savings for governments because they have to spend much less on tax collectors and taxation departments. The exorbitant amounts that will be saved will then be able to be better spent on areas governments are known to cut in their budgets: health care, education, and social work programs.

One of the cornerstones of Humanity's Bill of Rights is equality and fairness. These must be major factors in every aspect of any civilization humanity creates. If history has taught us anything, it is that something as simple as taxes can lead to civil unrest and discontent and can even topple governments. If any government worth its weight is going to prosper, taxation must be done equally and fairly, with all people being taxed at the same rate. Our leaders need to wake up to the fact that the unfairness they create by offering special benefits to their friends and the people who help fatten their wallets only leads to hate and discontent. Fairness and true equality in all aspects of government and humanity are the only things that can lead to the building of a society that can withstand the sands of time.

22 - RIGHT TO GATHER AND PEACEFULLY PROTEST

all people have the right to gather in groups and also to protest peacefully in all matters they see fit to do so for, as long as they do not infringe on the rights of others, including with harassment and bullying.

Look what happened when the employment law in France—the law was withdrawn because the people marched in the streets. I think what we need is a global protest movement of people who won't give up.

JOSÉ SARAMAGO

Two of the most powerful and effective ways in which humanity has instituted change have been through protesting and active speaking out. Some of the greatest changes and moments throughout our history have happened in large part due to people gathering and protesting. Time and time again, the sharing of ideas on these occasions has proven to be a great method of spreading knowledge and inspiring ideas for change. Humanity's history is filled with examples and lessons for all of us to learn from, from the era of absolute monarchs in Europe's past to modern-day marches and protests for rights and civil liberties.

One of my earliest memories of learning about protests was back in 1985 while watching an episode entitled "Tomorrow's children" from the television show "Fame" . The students in the show launched a protest by forming a sit-in that drew the attention of the media. I remember that during the episode they performed "The War Song," a song that had recently been released by Culture Club and which I developed an instant love for. The one scene from that TV show that has stuck with me even after all these years was when this lady sat on a stool in the middle of the student protest and sang a very heartwarming song titled "Blowin in the Wind". I later found out that this amazing songstress, Joan Baez, is a long time anti-war activist.

All of this was new to me when I saw it, so I asked my mom about it, and she spoke honestly with me. During the course of the evening, I learned about her own experiences as a witness to history. I also learned about the turbulent 1960s, Woodstock, hippies, civil rights, and many other things. All of these things and that one special evening had a lasting impact on my life. In my eyes, if characters on a TV show had the guts to stand up and speak out for what they believed in and one of the most loved bands of the time could create such a powerful song as "The War Song," there was nothing in this world I could not accomplish. Even though I did not have copies of those two glorious songs from that show to listen to, I still could hear them in my head loud and clear.

There is so much throughout humanity's history on this topic that it really is hard to find a starting point, so I sat down and spoke with my husband about it. He spoke about the gay rights movement and the beginnings of the Sydney Gay Mardi Gras. The modern gay rights movements started in 1969 with what is now known as the Stonewall Riots, when patrons of the Stonewall Inn, a popular mafia-owned hangout for gays and lesbians, fought back against the police persecution that was rife in the era. It was an era when police would raid bars if they simply did not like the people who were there, regardless of whether or not they were doing anything wrong. Well, one fateful night in 1969, the would-be victims fought back, and it sparked rioting and massive protests.

The brave stand those people took sent massive shockwaves through the United States and even the world, but nowhere were they felt more than in the gay community. Within a year, several organizations had been founded that were openly advocating and supporting the people of the gay and lesbian community. Newspapers were founded and began to openly print their news and other items of social importance. On the first anniversary of the Stonewall Riots, memorial marches were launched in many cities around the United States. One of the lasting impacts of that night in 1969 was that a people who had been hunted and marginalized were finally given a voice.

Many years later, on June 24, 1978, another major event like the Stonewall Riots occurred in Sydney, Australia. Originally, a group of protesters took to the streets to call for an end to discrimination of gays. The protest organizers were initially given permission to have the march, but that was later revoked and police force was called in. The protesters numbered somewhere in the range of at least one thousand people, with fifty-three of them getting arrested when police brutality was used to stop the protest.

I was fortunate to have had a chance to interview someone who was there that night. The Sydney of that era was one that was totally different from that of today. Homosexuality was illegal in New South Wales, and the police capitalized on that. They turned hunting down gays into a big business. Many cops lured and trapped many men, gay and straight, on trumped-up charges. They would catch people in public restrooms and ticket them on charges of lewd behavior, even though most were just there to do a bit of Mother Nature's business. Many people were tired of the wrongful police persecution and being treated like second-class citizens and so took to the streets in what started out as peaceful protest and ended with the police brutally attacking and arresting protesters.

The person I interviewed was like many that night: once the police started in, he, like everybody else, just took off running for his life. Also like many others, my interviewee had a job he could not risk losing. Being out at that time was unheard-of (and illegal, too). The events of that night greatly affected him: a week later he left Australia for Europe. He lived there in safety and was offered a level of security he could not have had in his own home country at that time. He did not call Australia home again for twelve years. When he returned, he returned to a country that was totally changed, due in large part to the events that took place in 1978 and the fallout from that night.

The main purpose of gathering and protesting is to advocate for change, and it is not hard to find the numerous examples of this, good and bad, throughout history and in our modern era. The 1960s in the United States were a turbulent time, with such events as the civil rights movement and the Vietnam War taking place. I was able to sit down and talk openly and honestly with both of my parents about this time in history. It was a violent time in the South as well as in many other places through the United States, which were filled with people who had long been neglected and were now fighting for equal rights. Many of them suffered greatly from everything from beatings and arrests to killings.

One of history's greatest and most respected men was most active during this era—Dr. Martin Luther King. The work he did inspired others, and he put himself on the line by choosing to stand up and make his voice heard. He was a great man with a powerful voice who spoke out against the injustices around him. One of his greatest speeches of all time was when he spoke from the very heart of the capital of the United States—the Lincoln Memorial—in 1963, during the immortal March on Washington. He delivered his "I Have a Dream" speech.

Another movement of the 1960s was the anti–Vietnam War movement. Hundreds of thousands of students and other people rejected the pile of bullshit they were being fed by the powers that were. While the United States was fighting a heartless war fueled by the bureaucrats and industrialists of the day, a new subculture developed and thousands dropped out of mainstream society and took to the streets with the sole purpose of stopping a war no one had any business fighting. I can speak firsthand on this topic because one of my father's brothers was killed in that conflict that so many were protesting about. I know how much psychological damage was done to my family. I am grateful to all those who did protest and speak out because I know many families were saved from the trauma that was needlessly inflicted upon my own family. My family is neither alone nor unique; we are but one of many.

I spoke with my mom about her life in the 1960s. She was raised in a small town in Louisiana, and the protests did not touch the people there. Life went along as normal, but she did mention one important bit of information that she remembers from the time. In high school, she became pen pals with several men in the military. There were ads in the papers encouraging people to write them. She exchanged letters with many of them, but every one of them was shipped to Vietnam. As soon as that happened, she never heard from them again and often wondered what happened to them. She may not have marched in the streets, but she was happy for those who did because they did their part to ensure that more lives were not lost to a senseless war.

One infamous example of people protesting for change occurred in Tiananmen Square in 1989, when a group of students demonstrated in a large prodemocracy movement. The protests made the news all across the globe, yet the Chinese government did everything in its power to stop and control the flow of information, even of the number of deaths that occurred due to the harsh and horrific approach taken to quell the protests. The protests had many impacts, but most were not good. China lost a lot of its reputation on the world stage. Those who were not murdered in the protests were hunted down. China even went after government officials who were sympathetic to the students' cause. Most of the people behind the protests were students who only wanted a better, more democratic future for themselves and who were just doing what they felt was right in order to accomplish that.

History as a whole is a large lesson in what people can accomplish with the power of protest. In the late 1800s and early 1900s, one of the most well-spoken protest movements happening was the women's suffrage movement. It became a movement when women stepped out of the kitchens and took to the streets to fight for the right to vote and to have their voices heard. The work those women did affects every facet of our lives today. They paved the way for women to gain power and step forth as equals of men and to relinquish their status as second-class citizens to be left in the kitchens and raising the babies.

Another powerful movement began in the early part of the 1900s that has continued at different points in time and places around the world. It was a movement that had never happened before on such a massive and widespread scale—workers' protests. They had happened before through-out history but never before with so much virility and passion. Around this time, unions formed in greater numbers than ever before. You had men, women, and even children taking to the picket lines and forcing the wealthy industrialists and bourgeoisie to wake up to the horrors they were creating with miserable working conditions and low, degrading pay for their employees. It is because of them that many workers now enjoy livable wages and many countries now even have minimum wage levels. Today, workers continue to protest in this manner. One recent example of this occurred in Australia, when people working for Qantas Airlines took to the picket line and actually caused major troubles for the entire airline.

Many great men and women who are now etched into the pages of our history books first rose to prominence because they dared to speak out in protest of what they felt was wrong. Gandhi, Martin Luther King Jr., Nelson Mandela, Susan B. Anthony, Elizabeth Cady Stanton, César Chávez, Rosa Parks, and Larry Townsend—all of the people on this list, in addition to the many others whom I have not named, all sacrificed themselves to fight injustices on many fronts. The realms they covered are numerous and include civil rights, women's rights, gay rights, workers rights, and more.

If we are to talk about the power of protest and what it can accomplish, though, we must also talk about the dark side of protesting. This dark side I speak of includes many thoughtless and heartless acts committed due to selfishness and greed and without proper regard for the lives and rights of others. Rioting, bombings, and hunger strikes are just a few of the types of protests that have their roots in this dark side. One the most memorable occurrences of this kind of protesting is one that I was a witness to—the LA riots of 1992. Four policemen in Los Angeles had been acquitted of beating a black man, despite a videotape showing the entire ordeal go down. Many angry people took out their frustrations in the worst ways possible—by rioting, looting, and burning and destroying property. It has been reported that at least fifty-three lost their lives in the riots and thousands of others were injured. I will never forget any of this because I remember vividly one Friday afternoon at my own high school when a race riot broke out. The people involved were students who had gone to school with each other for many years but who had suddenly started beating the shit out of each other for no good reason. That was really one of the saddest days I can remember being a witness to.

History can be a great teacher to us all. It can teach us the lessons learned by others in many areas of their lives and even show us the power of what gathering and protesting can accomplish. If we are to continue to grow and prosper, we must allow all voices to be heard. Many times in the past and in the present, people have fought for their rights. Sometimes it has been as simple as holding a protest march or a sit-in, and other times it has been as vile as a bombing. I believe people must be heard, but any form of protest that violates any of the rights of others is not worth even being around. Fight for what you believe in, but harm none in doing so.

23 - RIGHT TO OWN AND OPERATE A BUSINESS

no one, regardless of any factors, shall be prohibited from owning and operating a legal business of his or her choosing. Also, all fees related to owning and operating a business shall be reasonable and fair, so that running a business is accessible to all people.

a business has to be involving, it has to be fun, and it has to exercise your creative instincts.

RICHARD BRANSON

Businesses of every shape, size and type are the current cornerstones of life for all of humanity's children. If we are to have healthy economies that can fully support the people of humanity and their children, no one must be excluded from owning and operating a business. There are many places in the world where people are discriminated against in the business world. The most commonly discriminated against are females and racial minorities. I am not just talking about one country in particular where this happens, because there are countries all over the world on almost every continent where discrimination proliferates in the business world.

Many countries also use bureaucracy and laws to hold people down and to stop certain people from running businesses. These restrictions include the outright banning of people from owning businesses, the denial of business licenses, hefty taxation, the use of scare tactics, the changing of laws, and the implementation of rezoning laws, among many others. If a government wants to stop someone from having a business, it will find any way to do so, legal or illegal. Many groups will go so far as to use religion and theology to keep people from pursuing their own business ventures.

Any government worth its weight and that wishes to ensure its own financial freedom and future must allow free enterprise and business to grow and prosper. All businesses must be taxed evenly and fairly and not in a manner that will cause financial harm to the businesses. All governments must ensure the safety and rights of all workers. Governments must ensure all businesses pay fair and livable wages and that laws are in place to protect the health and welfare of the people, and they must provide checks and balances for businesses.

The businesses of humanity are indeed some of the most vital resources for our economies and livelihoods. However, a wise man once said, "With great power comes great responsibility," and nowhere else is that more applicable than in the world of business. All businesses must treat their employees and workers with dignity and respect. They must also uphold all of Humanity's Bill of Rights. They must provide safe working environments and conditions for their people and be willing to offer proper care for the times when their workers are injured or harmed in the course of employment.

Businesses must also respect and care for the lands and environments they use in the course of their business endeavors. The environment is only theirs to borrow, not to rape and pillage and then be thrown away. Throughout history and even into our modern era, many businesses act with no regard for the environments they operate in. Rivers, lakes, and waterways around the planet are polluted to the point where many are suffering environmental collapse of their ecosystems. Millions of people across the planet live in contaminated areas because of the greed and heartlessness of businesses, big and small.

One of the greatest tragedies caused by a business occurred in the Gulf of Mexico, which suffered the largest oil spill in human history. The Gulf oil spill is one that hit very close to home for me because I grew up in the bayous of Louisiana, the same bayous now critically endangered because of the oil spill. I know many people personally whose lives have been affected by this tragedy, but they will never see any compensation for the burdens and troubles they now deal with in the wake of this mess. For generations, many people have lived along the bayous and coasts. They have built many different businesses that cover a wide range of services and needs, but now many of them are either closed or endanger because of the carelessness of a major global corporation. This is one of many environmental disasters to make its dirty mark on our world, and those are two of many species to suffer needlessly at humanity's hands.

People must be allowed to earn a living and to open and run the businesses of their choosing. We must finds ways to allow people to pursue dreams and allow everyone to pay and equal share of taxes. They must be allowed to pursue their goals and dreams, without having the government treat them like a cash machine or a tax pit. One of the areas of government the world over where people complain about is being over-taxed. Whether it is true of not, it clearly shows us that things do need to change and improve. The governments of humanity must do their part to support them and also to support the workers of those businesses. Businesses and governments must also realize that they are not above the people but are rather of the people and must act accordingly. Businesses must also keep in mind that the people and environments of humanity are not theirs for the raping but that these things are instead only theirs to borrow.

24 - SEPARATION OF CHURCH AND STATE

no governing body shall make laws based upon religious doctrine, and every governing body shall always maintain a clear line between the them, without the policies of one affecting or influencing the other.

I'm completely in favor of the separation of Church and State. My idea is that these two institutions screw us up enough on their own, so both of them together is certain death.

GEORGE CARLIN

had a strong Catholic upbringing, but as I grew older, I made my own choices about my beliefs and how I would express them. I was lucky to be born in a country that allowed me the freedom to live my life according to my own choosing and to go about expressing my beliefs however I liked, rather than in a country that demanded a certain level of religious devotion or made me choose a belief system I did not feel was my own. I believe religion gives us a certain moral basis on which we can build and live our lives, but I do not believe it should be involved in any way in the manner in which a government leads its people or that a government should be leading a church.

There has been much talk in the news recently about governments based on religious doctrine, but what many do not realize is that it is actually a very old topic and one that has been around for many years. One of the oldest religion-based governments to come to mind was that of Emperor Caligula of Rome. During that time in history, Rome was still a country whose main religion was based around many gods and goddesses, although a small sect called Catholicism was gaining followers. Members of this new sect were persecuted, jailed, and even killed for their beliefs. They practiced their beliefs underground for fear of death or worse at the hands of what history has labeled "the mad emperor."

During Europe's long era of monarchies, the church held much power throughout Europe, so much so that it was able to launch many great persecutions, such as the Medieval Inquisition, the Spanish Inquisition, the Portuguese Inquisition, and the Roman Inquisition. These inquisitions ruined many lives and saw many people tortured, arrested, and even killed, compliments of the leaders in power. Most of these saw many non-Catholics, such as Jews, Protestants, and Muslims, hunted and persecuted for their beliefs. They were forced to either accept the Catholic beliefs forced upon them or suffer. In these dark times, many historic religious documents and buildings were destroyed.

In our own times, we hear much in the news about countries that have based their own systems of law and justice upon Sharia law, a system that has its basis in Islamic law and teachings. Although it varies by the country, this basis denies many people the right to make choices in their lives and openly discriminates against those who oppose the law or whose beliefs do not fit with this one narrow-minded view. It is not a coincidence that in all the countries that have Sharia law in place, those who identify as homosexual face some of the toughest legal penalties on the planet. In addition, these are also countries where women find themselves with the least amount of rights and lowest social standing.

There are many countries throughout this world of ours that without enacting Sharia law still use religious beliefs to define their legal systems; this oppresses and discriminates against many people and denies many their rights. Currently in the United States, the Republican Party has taken a religious route and is trying to undermine the rights of others by forcing its members' beliefs on everyone with its political influence. They are even going so far as to rewrite history by stating that the United States needs to go back to the Christian values it was founded on. What a load of horseshit. The United States was founded by a bunch of businessmen who wanted to have a fair say in how they were taxed and treated. It was those Founding Fathers who even saw fit to institute the separation of church and state as an ideal because, at the time, rule in England was still very heavily influenced by the church (the monarch of England is, after all, considered to be the head of the Church of England).

If we turn back the pages of history, there are two men who stand out in the fight for separation of church and state—Thomas Jefferson and James Madison. These men, with the support of many others, established this separation at a time when religion ruled many lives, including the lives of those in power. James Madison was quoted is 1811 as saying, "Practical distinction between Religion and Civil Government is essential to the purity of both, and as guaranteed by the Constitution of the United States." In 1822 he went on to further say, "We are teaching the world the great truth that Governments do better without Kings and Nobles than with them. The merit will be doubled by the other lesson that Religion flourishes in greater purity, without than with the aid of Government."

I could sit here all day going through the pages of history of many countries and pointing out the reasons why humanity needs to keep its governing bodies and religious beliefs separate, but the fact of the matter remains—most religions practice discrimination and violation of many human rights. Religion can help give us a moral basis on which we can build, but in the end the free will of the members of humanity must be allowed to reign. A simple and effective way to build fair and equal governing bodies is to base them upon Humanity's Bill of Rights and to ensure equality, justice, and fairness for all people; that includes allowing those who have their religious beliefs to enjoy them but also allowing those who choose another to enjoy that as well.

IN CLOSING

Life's not worth a damn
Till you can shout out—I am what I am.

GLORIA GAYNOR, FROM THE SONG "I AM WHAT I AM."

Who we are, who we become, and who we strive to be is passed upon our past, present, and our future. Our past is our educator. It teaches us lessons from the good and bad alike. It can be so powerful of a force that it evens leads us forth in our lives. Our present is that in which we live. It is where our past had lead us, but with a future that has yet to be written. Our present should always be known as the place in which we make our own choices to decide our future. We can make our futures be anything we want. If we take the time to learn from the lessons of our past without carrying its baggage, we can achieve many mighty things.

I believe that humanity has yet to come into its full potential as a species; as the true rulers and guardians of the planet Earth. If we are to do this, then we must do so with love, respect, and dignity for all members of humanity and its children. Although now we call this wonderful planet Earth our home, our species may one day take to the stars and make its mark upon other worlds, but that does not matter because we are now and always will be equal. One day down the road, our species may even evolve, with Mother Nature throwing in even more interesting variations of humans and their offspring. But no matter who you are or where you come from, every person deserves nothing more than another.

Because of our genetics as a species, we have taken many different forms and are composed of widely original individuals who make up the countless cultures, tribes, and social groups of humanity; though different, every person is just as worthy as the person standing next to them, and each deserves the same, nothing more and nothing less. We need to respect that diversity that makes us so wonderful, so varied, and so unique.

Humanity has been dividing itself based on its petty differences instead of embracing them, and in doing so humanity has also raped, pillaged, and mutilated our home, the planet Earth. Our home planet is in dire straits; many species of planets and animals are already gone forever, and many more are endangered. We are destroying the very biodiversity that helped propel us as a species. We are reaching a critical point in our own evolution and survival as a species, and if we do not alter our path now and fast, we may see our own oblivion.

It does not have to be that way. We have the brains and skills needed to not only save our species and our home planet but also to propel ourselves forward into uncharted territories of life and space. I do not think it to be inconceivable that we may one day make new homes for humanity on other worlds and take with us the wisdom to safeguard those homes from the destruction and devastation we have so far inflicted on our fellow members of humanity and our home.

Throughout all of my journeys, the one thing I have found every person I have met wants is to make the most out of their life and to be given a fair chance. We all want a chance to be able to take care of ourselves. In Australia, there is a very popular saying: "a fair go." This is an idea that many Aussies live by that simply put allows people a fair chance. It is a simple concept that works very well in Australia and could easily work in every corner of the globe. In fact, why don't we try it? Everything we have tried up to now has failed. Look around: people are constantly trying to screw others over in order to make their own patches of existence better, without regard for the people they hurt who have the same rights and privileges as they do.

I am not going to sit here and say I have all the answers—in fact, that would be far from the truth—but I do believe that Humanity's Bill of Rights is indeed something we all need. By *all* I mean every member of humanity and the children who spring forth from it. Let us work to build our lives, societies, and civilizations upon these twenty-four simple, yet powerful, pillars. These pillars can help to light the way to one of humanity's brightest eras, an era I would love to live in and be a part of.

Everybody wants to be loved,
Everybody wants to be respected,
And everybody and I do mean everybody
Wants to be happy.

RUPAUL, FROM THE SONG "HAPPY"